An Educated Opinion

Veteran journalist turned vice president of a fortune 500 company Julia Harwell Segars understands Alabama culture the way George Wallace understood its politics. Need a manual to help you with the baffling, sometimes devious twists and turns of Southern mores? Look no further than *Aunt Sister*. Whether sports, holidays, religion, bidness, food, travel, manners, family and more ... you'll find perfect descriptions of all familiar — and some heretofore unfamiliar — Alabama traditions, written in an original and comic prose. *Aunt Sister* not only knows the difference between a real neighbor and a "waving neighbor," she also nails pre-pubescence. It's when "The boys' voices hadn't changed and neither had the girls' chests." Pearls like these are on nearly every page of this 184-page book. If you're native to our region, you'll want to get your copy of *Aunt Sister* immediately to make sure you're, well, abreast of all things Alabama. And if you're from up North, in the words of the classic commercial, don't leave home without it.

Ed Mullins, 8/29/17
Retired Dean,
College of Communication
and Information Sciences
The University of Alabama

Aunt Sister

Julia Harwell Segars

Bless your ♡ !

julia h. segars

ISBN: 978-0-692-94633-6

Published by
Segars Creative, LLC
1 Bristol Place
Anniston, AL 36207

Cover and interior design by Bill Adams, Potts Marketing Group, LLC
Illustrations by Chris Harris and Bill Adams

Published in 2017

Printed in United States of America

For Franklin,
who keeps me in the road and points me forward.

Acknowledgements

I may have, sooner or later, gotten around to putting together a book of the best of Aunt Sister – assuming she was still alive and kicking for a few seasons after her column debuted in February 2016. But I would never have gone almost immediately into book mode without the early urging of Tom Potts, owner, and Bill Adams, creative director, of Potts Marketing.

They saw the potential in our aunt for a broader audience from the first time I sent them the link to the online version of the column in the Talladega Daily Home.

They also have been my co-conspirators on all aspects of this venture – from logo and book design and production to marketing across traditional and social media platforms – not only for the book itself, but for all things Aunt-Sister-related, both present and future. What a long, strange and fun trip it's been, and we're just at mile-marker 57.

Bill also collaborated with artist Chris Harris on the illustrations, little gems that punctuate each spread with a minimalist grace as a counterpoint to my sometimes over-the-top text. Yin and yang.

A huge thanks, as well, to Robert Jackson, publisher of the Talladega Daily Home (among his other titles at Consolidated Publishing); and to Anthony Cook, editor of the Daily Home, for allowing me the space and freedom to have some cloak-and-dagger fun under the guise of my alter ego while keeping it separate from my paying career.

My two editors-in-chief – father Hoyt Harwell (retired Associated Press correspondent), and daughter Emily Thomas (communications specialist at a major Atlanta institution) – have saved me from innumerable missteps in editorial content. Not much gets past their four blue eyes.

Emily also has been of tremendous help in shaping book content, including column selection, chapter order, character development and overall tone, and in helping the rest of the Aunt Sister marketing team (all over 50) understand and navigate the social media universe to ensure stickiness in that space. I am in awe of my red-headed wunderkind.

To Andy Norwood, I owe my next child (empty promise, and both of us are good with that) for invaluable legal advice and assistance. I'll at least buy you a Billy the Kid Burger and a Coke for old times. Maybe even some fries.

To my family members and dear friends who have (and will continue to be) inspirations for Aunt Sister characters and stories, I appreciate beyond measure your willingness to be good sports about all this foolishness. Y'all make it real.

To my dear husband, Frank, thanks for loving me and having faith in me through the exploration of one crazy-ass idea after another, whether it amounts to something worthwhile or a junk pile in the basement. Swing time is the best time of all.

And finally, to everyone who has bought this book or has read the column and come back for more, all I can say is "Bless your heart."

Table of Contents

FOREWORD

Aunt Sister was her familial name. She was my grandfather's sister. But it wasn't until I read the program at her funeral did I realize that Aunt Sister had a real name – a real Christian name and an absolutely beautiful name at that – Julia Adolyn. With such a gorgeous double name, why would you allow yourself to be called "Sister"? We Southerners don't have a choice really.

And then, as nieces and nephews came along, familial titles were added to the nickname, and she became "Aunt Sister" proper. As time goes on, one's given name takes residence in the shadows and one's nickname takes precedent – until a legal document needs signing or an obituary is written.

You don't get to pick your nickname – the family does. And it will follow you to elementary school and beyond. When one is given a nickname, one must own it. The nickname takes on a persona of its own and grants the recipient power and privilege to use the nickname as a stage name in this Southern drama we call life.

So when my cousin Julia Harwell Segars adopted Aunt Sister as her stage name for penning these columns, she winked at our shared lore while deftly capturing the broader heritage that is All Things Southern.

In my day job as a designer, I try to uphold that heritage as well. I also try to impress my clients with words they may not know or understand. As Aunt Sister points out in "Wearing the Sling of Outrageous Fortune," I used this technique on her, too. While she may have gotten injured on her do-it-yourself job, at least her back yard looks mighty fine with its parterre!

As Southerners, we have learned that to successfully get through this life, one must laugh to keep from crying. In "I love you." "You're welcome.", Aunt Sister recounts the tragic loss of her brother with a delicate dose of humor that does not bely the grief beneath the surface.

It reminds me of my experience when saying goodbye to my mother. On the day of Mama's visitation, we could have used some of those "toters" mentioned in "Send-Offs with A Six-Pack." The place was full. Everyone in town was there – everyone except my mother!

An ice storm, a coroner with the flu and a series of unfortunate events led Mama to be late to her own funeral. However, none knew the wiser; and honestly, would anybody be shocked that Jeanie Granade Farmer was late? My siblings and I shared a little chuckle as the guests told us, "We know your mama isn't here – we know she's with Jesus." If they only truly knew!

A nickname is the entre to a story. Just like a recipe. If I asked you for a pound cake recipe, your first response wouldn't be, "How many cups of sugar?" It would be, "When Mama did it, she..."

Our Aunt Sister was full of stories. I bet you have an "Aunt Sister," too – an elder member of your clan to celebrate, emulate and – due to genetics – probably transform into, whether you like it or not. You may even be a namesake.

Generations to come may be born Julia Adolyn, but called "Sister," or Puff, Dixie, Boo, Minnie, Mimi, Cap'n, Beau or Shug. May they live up their names, and may their nieces and nephews commemorate them, too, through written word – what a legacy!

James T. Farmer, III
May 2017

INTRODUCTION

About 18 months ago, I was holding onto the frazzled edges of sanity – ok, I was just a bit stressed with work and life in general, but hyperbole is more fun – and I needed a creative outlet to help the synapses fire and hit their mark.

I missed writing, my first calling, and so approached friends in the newspaper business to see if they would be interested in publishing a humor column if I were to write one. Those friends knew my ancient background (journalism degree, newspaper reporter, corporate writer, etc.), and I had written a couple of travel pieces for them in the past, so they didn't cock their heads in confusion at the idea. Besides, I was free.

Although I tend to see humor and irony in most everything, I had never attempted humor writing as a genre. But given my very public day job, I needed to stay away from opinion pieces and didn't have time to do any feature writing that required real legwork and interviewing.

I agreed to put together a couple of pieces for the editors to "kick the tires;" and in turn, they agreed to publish my offerings under a pseudonym. I did not want any issues arising from this venture to trespass across the border of my real job, which was putting real kids through college and real food on the table.

And, thus, Aunt Sister was born. Actually, she was resurrected. Growing up, I had an Aunt Sister. She was my mother's sister Julia Adolyn, and her siblings called her "Sister" growing up. It stuck, and when the next generation came along, she became Aunt Sister to us. It was so Southern, and since my name is Julia, too, a great inside joke for me and the clan.

The first couple of columns were rants – (see Purple Pill Blues) – but I soon got them out of my system and settled down to write more about family, current life experiences and memories of growing up on The Mountain.

The stories, to date, are mostly true, but with Aunt Sister telling the tales, they took on a life of their own. As friends began to suspect the identity of the author, I started winking at it myself. Ok, so I regularly posted the column link on my Facebook page.

However, I will not admit to being Aunt Sister. She is a part of me, and I am a part of her – but she has evolved into a voice of her own, sometimes bolder than I, sometimes more subdued. It depends on subject matter and our comfort level with it.

I've been pleasantly surprised by Aunt Sister's prolific nature. She has more story ideas than time to write them. It's also been amazing to watch her voice blossom from Minnie Pearl corn pone to the more thoughtful – and funny – voice of a modern Southern woman dealing with all that life throws her way, including sadness and grief.

Many of these pieces have been tweaked from the versions printed as a newspaper column, but more than a few are new material exclusive to the book. I hope you enjoy reading them as much as I have enjoyed channeling this sassy Southern Lady, who invites you now to go fetch a Mason jar of your favorite iced beverage, take a long sip and turn the page.

FREQUENT FLIERS

(Cast of Recurring Characters)

Aunt Sister: Our narrator and arbiter of Southern graces. Aunt Sister is a dab past 50, survivor of a long corporate career, mother and kick-ass grandmother. She has seen a lot and now lives to tell it, without too much fear of offending or reprisal. She appreciates good manners, good humor and good people. She'll suffer a fool, but not for too long. She believes in Jesus and big hair. A right-brained lefty, she is prone to bone-headed goofs. But she is the first to laugh at herself, and she freely confesses her failings. They make for good copy.

Fred: Aunt Sister's husband of 20-plus years. He loves his family, fishing and football. Fred occasionally combusts with firecracker fits of temper that are short-lived and serve to amuse his less-excit-able wife, who has dubbed them "Fred Fits." A killer griller, Fred lives to feed people and critters; and to organize; straighten; and balance his checkbook to the penny. A great Saturday for Fred "is to have good sex and then assemble a big piece of equipment with no parts left over. It's a guy thing," he explains. Fred has raised four children, two since birth and two more since they were youngsters. They all consider him Dad.

Little Darlin': Aunt Sister's daughter and older child by her first marriage. In her mid-20s, Little Darlin' is lightning in a bottle, flashing with red hair and verbal brilliance. She is a poster child for the benefits of a liberal arts education, thriving in a large city. She is a vagabond who has friends across the globe. Her home library (bedroom floor) is full of classics that she really has read, and her shelves are stacked with vintage albums of Miles Davis, David Bowie and a touch of Barry Manilow. LD bleeds for the world. She is the conscience of her family. They need all the help they can get.

Golden Boy: Nicknamed by his older sister, Golden Boy is the All-American kid who seems to have it all. Truth is, he works hard to make all that "luck" fall into place. GB lives to compete and to win. His humor is dry, and his temperament is calm on the surface. But those who know him well know that his feelings run deep and his thoughts deeper. He can figure out complicated algorithms for Fantasy Football and win big at Black Jack, but changing a tire stumps him. He is in his early 20s, and ready to tackle the world.

Mother/Bebop: Aunt Sister's mother, and a force of nature. The youngest of 10 from a hard-scrabble farm family in South Alabama, Bebop married young and got the hell out of Dodge. She had three children by age 25, then went on to a make it big selling real estate. Of Scottish and French descent, Bebop puts great stock in genes, manners and correct grammar. She is a bit high-strung, and her sharp wit and commanding presence forge into a cult of personality that draws legions of admirers. Her titanium exterior melts butter-soft in the glow of her seven grandchildren.

Daddy/Granddaddy: Aunt Sister's father. The oldest son of a Baptist preacher, Daddy is a Biblical scholar, sought-after Sunday School teacher and lexicographer. But true to the PK (preacher's kid) stereotype, he has been known to host the diaconate at weekly poker games after prayer meetings. Daddy's dry wit is legendary, as well as his knowledge of Alabama sports history and Southern politics. In his mid-80s, Daddy's morning routine includes completing the daily crossword puzzle with a pen and holding court over coffee with the "Piddlers" at his church of 50 years.

Big G: Aunt Sister's older brother, and polar opposite in many ways. He is neat, structured, punctual and sees the world in black and white. He is smart and literal-minded like his grandmother, Miss Genie. Mother says of them both, "If you tell them it's raining cats and dogs, they'll go get an umbrella." He found his niche professionally as an information technology specialist – a perfect job for a detail-oriented person who is great at customer service and closing the deal. Big G is the kindest of the three siblings, a wonderful father, great reader, craft beer enthusiast and true aficionado of rock music and University of Alabama football.

James: Aunt Sister's younger brother and kindred artistic soul. A songwriter and poet, lover of good literature and quiet moments in his study with his guitar, James conversely was at home on a stage in front of thousands or in a living room. True to his youngest-child birth order, he was famous on the mountain for his pranks and was a child at heart until the end. Husband, father, deacon and successful business leader, James was in the center of whatever was going on at church, in the community or in his profession. He found being a people magnet both exhilarating and exhausting. His family knows he is looking down on them from heaven and smiling at all the drama.

Gina Marie: Aunt Sister's partner in much middle-aged, manicured crime, and a true character in her own right. Gina Marie attracts men like tire-swing water draws mosquitos. She is funny most of the time, whether she means to be or not. Her long-winded descriptions of her life adventures are full of detours and made-up words that usually end in "thingy." But if you have the time to listen, she will eventually come back to the main road, and your belly will be tight from laughing during the trip. Gina Marie's aw-shucks veneer disguises a very savvy brain. She loves big and is a forever friend.

The Right Rev. Dr. James A. Mootauchy, Jr.: The long-time pastor of Aunt Sister's childhood church. Now retired, Brother Jim – like Daddy – is a fixture on The Mountain. He still preaches most Sundays somewhere, and his funeral services side business is thriving. Many of his A-grade sermons left lasting impressions on Aunt Sister, whether he knows it – and wants to take credit for it – or not. He has a down-home sense of humor, but takes seriously his calling to bring souls to The Lord. God bless him.

The Mountain: The community where Aunt Sister grew up and returned to live for many years. Its first residents, the rich steel barons of Birmingham, built summer cottages on its crest for their families as a way to enjoy fresh, cool breezes before air conditioning changed everything. It now has a good mix of blue- and white-collar residents, but not too many rich folks. It has sovereign citizens living down the street from liberal (relatively speaking) college professors. It has its share of "tetched" folks. It's both small-town and resort, with a thriving local hardware store and several mom-and-pop cafes. It has more churches than people; and, of course, The Pig.

"The only way you can describe a human
being truly is by describing his imperfections.
The perfect human being is uninteresting…
It is the imperfections of life that are lovable."

Joseph Campbell
The Power of Myth

"I spoke up this morning
This is what I said
'Glad to finally meet you
You people in my head'"

James Harwell
All I Need

"Our family members are all assorted nuts,
but not your garden-variety peanuts or pecans.
We are of the exotic Macadamia persuasion.
And salty, especially the women."

Aunt Sister

An Appointment to Fib

I learned to fib early in life. My mama taught me.

In addition to God and family, there were a few other things Mother held dear – they included good manners, good grooming, Tuesday and Friday hair appointments and her Sunday afternoon nap.

The good manners rules included the requisite Southern "ma'am" and "sir" responses to adults, particularly our parents; no gum-chewing in public, particularly in church; "please" and "thank you" as bookends to permissions granted; and the opening of car doors for girls and women, particularly her.

If my father was driving, he always opened the door for her. If the privilege was bestowed on one of my brothers, they usually remembered. If they didn't, her fanny would sit in that car until she died of heat stroke or hypothermia before she opened her own door. They rarely forgot.

Good grooming generally had to do with not being sloppily kempt or smelly. Mother did not approve of our looking, or acting, "common." That really wasn't a problem. Our family members are all assorted nuts, but not your garden-variety peanuts or pecans. We are of the exotic Macadamia persuasion. And salty, especially the women.

All the grandkids called our oldest aunt, Lorraine, "Aunt Nasty." You can imagine why. She embraced it. I should add that Aunt

Nasty was just as sweet on the inside as she was crusty on the outside. She just didn't want anyone to know it.

On the grooming front, our hipster, late- '70s teen-aged years just about did Mother in, bless her heart. But she learned to pick her battles with the hormones. She gave in to sloppy dress and settled for clean bodies, clean teeth and clean, long hair. And good posture. If you slumped your back, you got a gentle whack between the shoulder blades. "Stand up straight," she'd say. "Slumping is common."

The 9 a.m. hair appointments with Annette were carved in stone for at least 20 years. But they were worth the investment. A tall, stylish woman, my mother turned the heads of men young and old. She still does. When she recently retired at 76, she cut her hair appointments back to once a week. That had to hurt, bless her heart.

Then there were the legendary Sunday afternoon naps. After a whirlwind morning of Sunday school and church, and a big Sunday dinner of "rice, roast 'n gravy," Mother would retire to the green-tufted sofa in the den, cover up with a blanket and sleep on her tummy for two hours, minimum. We knew better than to disturb her. She earned that one afternoon of peace every week, given her full-time jobs as a successful Realtor, mother and wife.

But as a Realtor, she was subject to calls from agents, buyers and sellers all hours of the week and weekend. She drew the line on Sunday afternoon calls, and we were her first line of defense. She couldn't bring herself to ask us to flat-out lie as to her whereabouts, and napping would not have deterred many of the callers. So, she came up with a creative solution. She christened the green sofa "Appointment."

Thereafter, anytime anyone would call on a Sunday afternoon and ask, "Is your mother home?", we would answer with utmost politeness and in all truth, "She's on Appointment. May I take a message?"

No one's feelings got hurt or panties got wadded, and Mother got her beauty rest. We got a two-hour window for gum chewing and slumping. All in all, a little fib in the right situation can be a good thing, y'all.

The Purple Pill Blues

The trauma is real. My Little Purple Pill is now white. White. Like all the other unsexy pills of the generic or over-the-counter persuasion we take to keep the effects of acid, anxiety, bloating, blah, blah, blah, from ruining our day and belying our age.

I want my Little Purple Pill to be, well, purple. Not to be confused with the Little Blue Pill so popular with men, but just about as expensive. As a woman of a certain age, I liked popping a handful of miracle drugs in the morning with the color-coded assurance that all the right meds were in the daily dispenser. It's now an ordeal.

At least the drug makers choked on enough expense to put a shine to the fish-belly-white coating on my purple pill of yore. A fine, but critical distinction between it and the chalky white substitutes with which it shares space in my two-week dosage dispenser. But I still have to find my glasses when assigning each capsule to the right cubby hole in the dispenser.

And were it not for the gloss coating, I'd have to add at least two more precious minutes daily to convince myself that I had correctly dispensed all the dosages last Sunday. I'd hate to double up on regularity at the expense of reflux. These are real issues, people!

I love purple, and I really loved my purple pill. I feel cheated. The old bait-and-switch. Confidence men have done it since Jacob donned animal skins and stole Esau's birthright blessing right out from under blind Isaac's nose. The Devil made him do it. It's now called marketing.

Marketing drugs is the prescriptive cousin to Satan's sales pitch for his evil spawn, Spanx. Did you ever notice that if you gut the word Spanx, you have S_x? Fill in the blank with a vowel. Any vowel — Sax, Sex, Six, Sox, Sux... Now you have mood music, hanky panky, the Evil Number, more evil hosiery, and finally, a four-letter profanity, so to speak. But I digress.

Back to the drug pushers. I'm referring to the Madison Avenue beautiful people in all-black couture (none of whom need Spanx) who tell the rest of us — the hoards below — that it's fun to have toe fungus because it opens the door to that siren of scrips, Jublia. Jublia rolls off the tongue like jubilee and jambalaya. A party just waiting for some Cajun accordion music and tipsy guests armed for the throw-down with Little Blue and Little Purple Pills.

The other thing I really detest about Jublia, besides the animated toe that is its trademark, is its bastardization of a lovely Southern name. One of my best friends is named Julia. Now she sounds like a toe fungus, bless her heart. In fact, when I typed in Jublia for this column, AutoCorrect changed it to Julia. Her mother would be appalled.

I just want to go back to the good old days, when purple pills were purple, blue pills were not necessary, Spanx were a thing of the past that women had declared dead (think girdle), and

Julia was a perfectly respectable name for a perfectly respectable woman. Not a toe fungus.

The trauma is real.

Grandma Got Run Over
by a White Deer

I owe a big thank you to the gal holding number 09154. Because of you, I'm a winner.

It was one of those authentic small-town Southern ladies' luncheons in a church fellowship hall, resplendent with a "tablescape" contest, a fashion show, a nervous local speaker and so many door prizes that you had to be as unlucky as an albino buck on the first day of hunting season if your ticket wasn't drawn.

Call me Whitey the Deer.

Of the 240 attendees, about 10 of us remained prize-less when the drawing started winding down. The hostess called out another number, and one more desperate soul claimed her umbrella and rightful place in the hall of winners. Then, a silk flower centerpiece went to number 09245.

The lateness of the hour and beckoning appointments caused a trickling exodus of Spandex leggings topped with oversized tunics. One early departing soul, bless her clueless heart, was the bearer of ticket number 09154. The Voice called it out. Going once, twice, thrice. Elvis had left the building. There was still hope for the disenfranchised. "Number 09133," The Voice called.

"YEAH, Baby! That's me," I heard myself woo-hooing, as if I had won the mega Powerball lottery. I claimed my tiny Boston fern and my place on the Wheaties Box of Champions.

Why do we get so caught up in such stuff? It could have been a trip to Jamaica or a Happy Meal toy salvaged from a yard sale. Didn't matter. I needed to win. Men don't have a lock on testosterone moments. Now I don't have any chest hair to date, but it's not out of the picture.

"Successful competitors want to win. Head cases want to win at all costs," golfing legend Nancy Lopez once said. Yeah, sister, that's easy to say if you've won 48 LPGA tour events, including three major championships. I bet her mug graces a Wheaties box, too.

Head case, huh? Then scrap Whitey the Deer. Call me Psycho. Call all of us Belles psychos if there are prizes or deals to be had. Shopping for deals last week at a mega outlet, I heard my sweet girlfriend Gina Marie turn venomous. "Hands off the tree skirt, lady," she hissed at an elderly woman casually handling a clearance item Gina Marie had claimed in her treasure pile at the sales counter. She then laughed it off with a sugary "it's all in fun" comment, but we knew better. Those fangs had been ready to strike if necessary.

She didn't need a burlap tree skirt any more than I needed that fern. But, by golly, it's mine. It will be a colorful addition to the corporate-logoed plastic letter openers, back scratchers, cheap pens, t-shirts, Coke-can Koozies and tote bags that make up the mostly useless loot I've accumulated over the years. Most of it is cached in a plastic tub in the basement buried beneath long-abandoned Christmas decorations and un-shredded check stubs.

Someday, archeologists will root through the rubble among the ancient fern fronds and learn much about my disposable life and hoarding tendencies. But they won't find a Happy Meal toy. I may be compelled to win one, Psycho that I am, but I do have my standards. Our last plastic McDisney trinket went to the cemetery of broken commodes after our son Golden Boy dropped it in our cherished vintage aqua toilet 20 years ago, blocking all further discharges and enriching the coffers of a plumber. There is no love lost between me and a Lion King toy.

But that fern – that living proof of my raffle ticket prowess – has a home. At least until it dies of neglect while I'm scoping out a nail-grooming set that has my lucky number. Out of my way, Grandma! Whitey the Psycho Deer needs those clippers.

Minnows and a Marriage License: $11, Please

On a stretch of highway a few miles from home sits one of my very favorite brick storefronts, a local pawn shop. I love this shop because it says it all about life in the South. Old-fashioned hand lettering on the front of the building proclaims, "Jesus Saves." Then below it, in larger, bolder print: "We Buy Guns."

It's a one-stop shop for saving your soul and hocking your Glock. If the sign-painting owner is also a preacher, you could – one might surmise – have a true shotgun wedding on site. And if the gun gets fired (on purpose or on accident) during the I-Do's, he could preach a good funeral to boot.

We love economies of purpose in our retail establishments when we can't reach economies of scale. Big-box retailers who have figured out how to do both have made fortunes. While I'm not a fan of bigger-is-better stores, I do visit them on occasion out of necessity. But I always feel like I'm making a deal with the man below when I do.

My husband, Fred, is all about some volume and price deals, but he also is a firm believer in supporting the local economy when he can – especially when it comes with a little entertainment factor. One of his favorite Mom-and-Pops ever is the 'Leven-Dollar

Store. I don't remember the real name of the mercantile, but it is the local gas station/mini-mart that marks the end of civilization at the fork where a 10-mile dirt road continues the trek to our lake place.

"Every time I stop, the young lady at the counter always rounds the purchase price off to $11 because she can't do take-aways," Fred tells it. He usually adds that the clerk is easy on the eyes. That might explain her continued employment. If not, I'm betting she's related to the owner. In addition to her challenges with making change, her extremely long fingernails hamper her ability to ring up a purchase on the ancient cash register.

Fred occasionally takes a buddy with him to fish at the lake. One of his buds is my Uncle Napp, a retired preacher from Georgia. Fred had been telling Napp about the 'Leven-Dollar Store for some time, but Napp remained skeptical. If fishing tales had not been involved, the pastor might even have offered up an intercessory prayer to the Man above to help Fred change his lying, sinful ways.

That all changed after he and Fred made a stop at the fabled store. Napp was debating adding some beef jerky and a Moon Pie to the assortment of eggs, minnows, worms, potato chips and Co-Colas they had assembled for purchase. "I told him to put all of it on the counter. It didn't matter what he got. It would still be $11," Fred says.

So Napp did. The young lady looked at the pile and used the side of her right pinky to meticulously punch in a couple of prices. Then, true to her billing, she paused in utter futility, shrugged, and said sweetly, "That'll be 'leven dollars." Bless her heart. Uncle Napp burst out laughing. She just smiled back. Probably not the first joke she didn't get.

Every time we see him now, Uncle Napp asks Fred to tell the 'Leven-Dollar story. And Fred obliges, illustrating the pinky move at the appropriate juncture. Then Napp falls out laughing again.

If it were closer to his home, I believe Napp would make a daily visit to the 'Leven-Dollar Store just to witness the retail transactions. And while he was witnessing, he might could marry a few folks and bury a few others. It's the Southern way.

Big Blue was Good People

Other than growling a little when he was gassed, Big Blue kept his own counsel. That's saying a lot where I'm from – we call it "The Mountain." Like all Southern places where at least two are gathered, opinions on The Mountain are stronger than a high school boys' locker room after a ball game.

Most everybody knows where you stand on important things such as football, politics and religion. But Big Blue was different. He didn't practice what the Rev. Dr. James A. Mootauchy, Jr., aptly dubbed "Bumper Sticker Religion."

Blue's tailgate, though a lighter blue than the rest of him, was pristine of politics or preaching. He was a right genial fella, even for a truck. He was also the first to pitch in without complaint whenever a family member or friend needed his help.

He moved sofas and bed frames when kids moved out of -- or back into -- the nest. He hauled in sand, gravel and dirt; and he hauled out tree stumps and trash. My brothers used his horse-power to lug U-Haul trailers of band equipment to concert venues all over the Southeast, burning out two transmissions over time.

Big Blue was actually a 1982 Chevy Custom Deluxe Fleetside pickup, according to Fred's recollection of genus and species. It's important around here to know who your, umh, people are. Just plain pickup truck works for me. I was never one to dive into gene pools too deeply. Some are right shallow 'round here.

When Daddy bought Blue second-hand, he was a handsome dark blue with the chrome grill of a teenager. A trusting soul, Daddy always left Blue's doors unlocked with keys on the floor-board. Any friend was welcome to borrow him, as long as they brought him home when done.

That proved problematic only once, when Blue turned up missing for a week. (Yes, I know – "turned up missing" is an oxymoron.) After waiting several days with no sign of Blue, Daddy called the police and his insurance agent. About the time he hung up the phone, the truck reappeared in the driveway, without so much as a thank-you note or a "kiss-my-asphalt."

Daddy called off the search. "Several days later, an insurance man called and asked whether Blue had received any damage while on leave from our driveway," Daddy recalls. Because the adjuster's question failed to specifically link damage to just the most recent adventure, Daddy was tempted to mention all kinds of dents and dings that were already there. But he shooed the devil from his shoulder and stayed honest.

Daddy later found out who the borrower was, but he never told. The boy meant no harm. He just lacked manners.

During another overnight trip, this time to Mr. Bill's Service Station for maintenance, Blue suffered the indignation of a stolen tailgate, bless his heart. One of Daddy's buddies scavenged a light-blue replacement, but no one saw the need for matching paint. Thus, even more character was thrust upon our old friend.

Blue was a regular in the grammar-school carpool line when Daddy picked my kids up every afternoon. And, with his bed full of blankets, he hauled around our merry band of tone-deaf Christmas carolers every Dec. 23. We made a joyful noise, shall we say.

About 10 years ago, Daddy donated Blue to a charity that didn't care a wit if he was dinged, dented, overhauled and two-toned. Blue grumbled a bit when they gassed him up and drove him off, but I'm sure he didn't complain for long. Big Blue always kept his own counsel. He was a right genial fella, even for a truck.

On Bikes, Backsides and Birthdays

A few years ago, when I was being considered for an appointment to a public board, I had to first meet with a local official who didn't know me. After we visited awhile, chatting about issues of the day, he cut to the chase. "You're relatively young," he said, as if inspecting a horse's teeth.

Relatively young. Hmm. Compared to what? A stegosaurus? The pyramids? Grandma Moses? He meant it as a compliment, given that I was in my mid-40s. But it stung a bit. I called my dear friend Gina Marie, three months my junior, and informed her that we were, in fact, relatively young chicks. That became our mantra, and we're sticking with it, a decade later.

Men. Bless their hearts, they mean well. The delivery just goes ka-plewy sometimes.

Case in point: Two months before my big 4-0 – the one you typically go all out for with parties, balloons, diamonds, trips, etc. – my sweet Fred bought me a bicycle from Sears. I had mentioned that I wanted to start bike riding for exercise. Always encouraging of such behavior, he made sure it was a comfortable bike with an overly large seat. We jokingly called it the "big butt bike."

Fred is truly very thoughtful, and scored major points for the big butt bike, which he labeled an early birthday gift. We say that when we just want to give each other something for no occasion.

Fast forward two months, to the birthday weekend.... Complicating our situation is that Fred's birthday is the day after mine. We usually celebrate together with not much fanfare because he does not like the spotlight, and I am not overly high maintenance for a relatively young chic.

But 40 was The Year. It was supposed to be the big one. Although Saturday was the day before my official ascent to middle age, there was no surprise party, no big dinner. Nada. "Oh, I see," I thought. "He's going to drag out the anticipation all weekend and celebrate on Sunday afternoon."

When friends called by chance to see if they could come over Saturday afternoon and cut some hydrangea blooms from our backyard, I smelled the development of a surprise-party layup shot.

A little while later, my brother James called to see what we were doing for my birthday. In the course of the three-way conversation, I realized that nothing was on tap. Not even a family gathering. The hysterics that followed were epic.

Fred was dumbfounded. After all, he said, we never go big on birthdays, and he had gotten me a gift – remember the big butt bike? I was stunned. That's what every woman wants for her 40th – a bike that says, "Hey, you're relatively young, but if you sit your big backside on this baby and pedal hard, you can minimize the spread for a while."

Even higher-pitched wailing followed, at least until our friends came over with their pruners and bucket for the plant cuttings.

I snuffled up, splashed water on my mottled face and blood-red eyes and smiled the big fake smile all Southern women have in their tool kits. I welcomed our guests, who actually did come to cut flowers for an event they were hosting that night, not to fete me.

Digging out as quickly and as desperately as he could, Fred said to the unsuspecting friends, "My Sweetie's birthday is tomorrow. Can y'all go out with us and celebrate?" He put them on the spot for a dinner on a Sunday night. They didn't even have a chance for a private conversation to determine their interest. It was nigh-on pitiful. A free-throw from mid-court.

Trapped by Fred's "help-me-please stare," they agreed. We had a nice dinner the next evening at an okay chain restaurant, because, of course, no birthday-worthy five-star local restaurants are open on Sundays. Before the dinner, Fred sneaked out of the house and bolted to a mall jewelry store (again, limited options on Sundays) to salvage what he could of the day.

In the ensuing years, as many of our friends turned 40, whenever one spouse threw the big party or gave the big gift, I made sure Fred knew about it. Bless his heart, truly.

But, he does learn. Four years later, on our 10th anniversary, he arranged an overnight stay at a local resort, a lovely dinner with dear friends, and surprised me with the most beautiful mink coat a girl could hope for.

At least, a relatively young girl with a relatively normal butt...

Freudian Slips and Yosemite Flowers

AutoCorrect is the underwire bra of today's digital word – giving better form to poor writing and uplifting bad typists and lousy spellers to a higher plane of perfection.

But what a pain in the ribs! My experiences with the necessary evil app and its frequent misfirings have prompted me to dub it AutoCrap (copyright pending), with no affectionate undertones.

Recently, I was replying to a text from a co-worker named Cass. AutoCrap changed her name first to "Cast," and when I objected, went on to call her "Cyst." I'm okay with one "you-meant-to-type" auto correction, but at some point, the driver should have control of the wheel!

A text in which I intended to say, "No need to send flowers," somehow morphed to "Yosemite flowers." Now that makes so much more sense…

"Test" became "EDT," and "emergency" read "enemy hence." "Zone" became "she," "discontent" appeared as "dis into," and "like" became "lie."

So, if I didn't adjust my editing bra's hooks and straps, a message that I meant to read, "Cass: No need to send flowers over test results. No emergency. The results were in the acceptable zone. She is not discontent with them. Would you like to get dinner?"

Would, instead read, "Cyst: Yosemite flowers over EDT results. No enemy hence. The results were in the acceptable she. Zone is not dis into them. Would you lie to get dinner?"

Thanks AutoCrap, I'm sure that's what I meant to say. Well, I'll give you one -- knowing Cass, she might well lie and go bra-less to get dinner. Bless her heart. But, I digress. Or, as my good friend Miss Betty Baumgartner likes to say, I'm getting lost in the thicket of my secondary thoughts.

My secondary thoughts and misfiring neurons get me in enough trouble when I speak without AutoCrap weighing in when I write. I have been known to say "brump and booze" for "bump and bruise," "milthy finds" for "filthy minds," and "shared skit-less" for, well, you know…

Then there was "fragrant filtration" for "flagrant flirtation," and "ventless silence" for "senseless violence." Both smell of juvenile flatulence humor… Maybe a bit of Dr. Freud slipping in there?

My doctor says it's stress. I'll go with that. In fact, I occasionally find the slips more fitting than the intended words. It's the Dixie way. Ponder the Southern shortcuts that give us stand-ins for these longer word combinations: "tump" for "tip/tumble/dump," and "whup" for "whip/beat up."

Now consider these additions from my secondary thoughts to the primary lexicon: "froaming," for "frothing and foaming," "ver-brant" for "vibrant and verdant," and "fruss" for "fret and fuss." I heard this one at work last week: "dramastic," for "dramatic and drastic." Great word. Wish I had stammered into it first.

Here's a scary thought: Pair up an AutoCrap bra with a Freudian slip, and you might well get verbal lingerie that would make a Victoria's Secret model blush. But this is family reading, so I'll avoid flagrant flirtation with R-rated content that is dilthy and firty. I'll stick with good ole PG ventless silence.

Furbies Live to Haunt Again

My 21-year-old son, Golden Boy, sent a good-news, bad-news text to me late last year while Christmas shopping. "The good news is, I made an A on my exam. The bad-news: K-Mart has Furbies again."

Furbies haunted our home, and those of my two brothers, after our mother bought them en masse for all her grandchildren in 1998. Put to "sleep" at night on a bedroom shelf, a Furby would awaken when a child's bathroom trip triggered its motion sensor. The gremlin would open its creepy bug eyes, raise its eyebrows and move herky-jerky while spewing out "Furbish" words.

Their antics caused shrieks that shook the house and the nerves of all inside.

We turned them off. They still lived. We removed batteries to no avail. In our lucid hours, we attributed their immortality to some kind of battery charge storage thing-a-ma-jig, but our guts knew otherwise. They were spawns of Satan.

Much like Jimmy Hoffa, ours disappeared one day. Golden Boy and his big sister, Little Darlin', never asked what happened. We never told. My brother Big G smashed his kids' little fur devil with a hammer. Brother James drowned his Furby.

It wasn't until years later that we spilled the beans to our mother. We had not intended to confess and burst her bubble. She had braved the elements and the insanity of a pre-dawn Black Friday superstore line to buy them. She wanted her grandbabies to have the "It" toy that Christmas. Furbies first sold for around $35, but were soon going for $100 resale as demand outpaced supply. Enterprising capitalists sold them through newspaper ads and auctions for as much as $300.

The ironic thing was that none of our kids had asked for a Furby when my mother joined the 1.8 million frantic buyers in year one. By 2000, a reported 40 million had been sold. I have to wonder how many of those got the Hoffa treatment over time. I bet there is a Furby purgatory that resembles the Tower of Babel, given their Furbish-speak plus the 24 other languages they learned as markets grew global.

The demise of our Furbies came to light at a Christmas gathering a couple of years ago when we were going down memory lane. Our Furbies were merely Ghosts of Christmas Past. But once we leaked their fates, the kids made absolute family legend of them. They told of glowing Furby eyes staring at them from closet shelves in the wee hours while beaky lips called out their names.

Although Furby creators claim their speech is limited to programmed phrases, Little Darlin' swears that some of her Furby's language was not meant for young ears, having been picked up from the resident adults. Similar suspicions of their recording abilities caused the U.S. National Security Agency to briefly ban them from NSA offices in 1999.

By the time the grandkids finished their horror stories, their brushes with Furbies had warped them for life, much like their preschool encounters with the Crayola Easter Bunny, McGruff the Crime Dog and an automatic car wash.

It's a wonder any of us live to tell the tales of our youth. Maybe these 21st Century Furbies will pop open their android eyes and tell it for us.

Doppelgänger Gumdrops

Doppelgänger. How in the world did I live 50-plus years without rolling that incredibly rich word around my literary taste buds? It's almost as much fun to say as "chortle." When I finally did stumble across it, I saw and heard it everywhere – in print, on TV, on social media. It kept appearing, well, like a doppelgänger.

When I told Daddy I was devoting a column to doppelgängers, he asked, "So, you're writing about ghosts?" Darn his vocabulary. The man completes the Sunday New York Times crossword in ink, for Pete's sake.

Besides apparition, doppelgänger also means having a twin who isn't kin. Its roots are German, from "doppel," meaning "double," and "gänger," meaning "goer." Now in the South, not being kin on some level is a stretch. But I do have a doppelgänger, and to my knowledge, we're not blood. We really don't look much alike, but for some reason, people have confused us for years. My doppelgänger is my friend and former co-worker, Gina Marie.

Whether at work or social functions, people have sworn they saw me when it was Gina Marie, and vice versa. We finally learned to compare calendars when folks got us mixed up. It's not totally unfounded. We worked together several times over our careers, and have been friends for 25 years. Gina Marie is the kind of friend who knows what you're thinking before you speak. Most of the time.

One exception occurred a few months before the 2008 Summer Olympic Games. We worked with a young woman who had been a world-class long-jumper in college, and she got the opportunity to take a six-month leave from work to train and try out for the U.S. Olympic Track & Field Team.

Our star athlete came within a couple of inches of making the team on her try-out jump, and she returned to work understandably bummed. To cheer her up, we threw a welcome-home party in the office.

The local paper got wind of it and a sent a reporter/photographer to do a little feature. Because I was her boss, they wanted a quote from me. "We are so proud of Claire," I said to the reporter. "Two inches may not seem like much, but it is huge!"

When the words left my mouth, my stomach fell. The first rule in public relations is to keep it clean, or at least above locker-room humor even if the intent is honorable. I had been an official company spokesperson in prior years, so I knew better.

Gina Marie, another PR veteran, teased me without mercy. We both knew my ill-chosen words would raise the eyebrows not only of local readers, but also our corporate management. Our electronic clipping service was sure to carry it. Bless my heart.

So when I opened the newspaper the next morning and saw the quote, I fell out of my chair laughing. "Two inches is huge," it read, quoting our new area spokesperson, Gina Marie.

Lucky for us both, the corporate-powers-that-be either took no notice or let it pass. But Gina Marie was totally chagrined.

The sugar coating on that gumdrop was yet to come. Not too long after the incident, Gina Marie was invited to lunch by the elderly owner of the paper to welcome her to town and recruit her to Kiwanis.

When he dropped her off at our office afterward, he presented her with a laminated and framed copy of the Olympics feature. "I knew you would love to have a copy of your first-ever quote in our paper," he told her sweetly.

She chortled, bless her heart.

My doppelgänger never ratted on me. That's the way best friends are. Love you, Gina Marie.

Death Becomes Her

"Doesn't Cora Lee look natural?" I heard recently at a great-aunt's visitation. "She looks so peaceful."

Horse hockey. Aunt Cora Lee looked dead. No amount of Mary Kay foundation and pancake powder could pink up that gray pallor. Peaceful? Well, you may have something there. Cora Lee never got a moment's rest when she was alive, bless her heart. Uncle Pugh kept her hoppin'. Needy old coot.

Few things in life scare me as much as one thing in death – specifically, being dead and on display.

It takes me a good hour now to evoke that "natural look" from my countenance using face paints. And there is more than a smidgen of living color primed into the canvas before I even start.

As for me, closed casket. Closed subject.

My friend Gina Marie has a more vainglorious plan for her remains. She has a bad case of urn-envy regarding several of my antique porcelain vases, and has told her children that I am "Keeper of the Urn" in which her ashes will reside. Assumptions of my charity aside, I'm quite all right with that. She doesn't want any 62-year-old male mortician doing her hair and makeup, either.

Neither of us has an issue with death itself. Most Southerners don't. We invite it to pull up a chair and visit a spell. Or, in the case of my friend Lulu's folks, hang out on the screened porch.

Lulu's grandparents, Mawmaw and Pawpaw McPherson, were Depression-era people known for their thriftiness. So when a family friend in the burial-plot business offered them a deal, they jumped on it.

The McPhersons got two plots at a local cemetery for the price of one, and did the pre-purchase about 10 years before they were in need. But wait, there's more. Their enterprising friend also mentioned a great deal on tombstones.

"We're ready to go," they told their children and grandchildren, after summoning them to a family meeting one afternoon.

"What do you mean, 'you're ready to go?'" Lulu recalls asking.

"Come outside with us," Pawpaw said, chest puffing with pride and emphysema.

There on the porch, in places of honor facing their two wicker rockers, were the tombstones. "They were engraved with all the important information," Lulu says. "Everything was on there but the death date, which they said was just a fill-in-the-blank when the time came."

Mawmaw and Pawpaw said it was morbid to pre-plant the tombstones on the empty graves. "That's just asking for trouble," Mawmaw said. She also thought it would be tacky to store them inside the house. But, Lulu explains, they wanted easy access.

"The only thing was, the porch was where they liked to smoke," she says. "So, they spent quite a bit of time out there. They weren't fazed by it at all."

Pawpaw's emphysema and a heart condition required him to be hooked up to an oxygen tank all the time. "Every day, he'd wheel it outside, turn it off and take his mask off long enough to chain smoke a few Camels while he stared at his own gravestone. We'd hear him coughing and laughing at the radio."

I think the McPhersons may have been on to something. Choosing my own headstone and crafting my own epitaph would keep others from doing unto me after I'm done. I might even relish the thought of actually getting to live a spell with the home décor of my final resting place.

Those left to manage the earthly details of my departure would only have to fill in the blank on my tombstone relating to the date that I found the need to officially use it. And, of course, to ensure adherence to my last wishes.

Closed casket. Closed subject.

Don't be Messin' with No. 2

"LOOK!" screamed the bold letters on the temporary sign posted at my favorite drive-thru. "Your meal number may have changed!"

"The horrors!" I thought. "Fire The Ronald." Oh wait, Mickey D's already dropkicked the clown. I guess their PR machine finally noticed all the red-nosed psychos popping up in the police blotter and on the big screen. That, or an image consulting firm got paid megabucks to polish up the Golden Arches.

I drove on through the queue to order. "Speak up so we'll know you're there," read a hand-written note taped below the menu. "Our sensor isn't working."

I quickly ordered the Diet Coke that is my guilty pleasure every afternoon. "Would you like a fresh-baked hot apple pie with that?" the server asked with rote pleasantness. I assured her that if I had wanted a fresh-baked hot apple pie, I certainly would have ordered one and saved her from worrying that I might. (After consulting with another outside PR firm, Mickey D's banished fried pies years ago for those oh-so-healthy baked ones.)

Soft drinks were on special for $1. Our local sales tax is 10 percent. I fished through my car change holder for the requisite $1.10. "That'll be... that'll be... oh, I'll have it figured out by the time you drive around," the attendant said sweetly, math anxiety flustering the spiel out of her. Bless her heart.

I drove on to the first window to settle up. "I'm here," the driver of the plumber's truck behind me yelled into the speaker. "Hello? Hello?"

I chuckled to myself, thinking about those pesky meal-number changes. That really would rock some worlds. Why in heaven's name would the burger chain rain this plague on both their customers and servers? I guessed the PR firm was at it again. Baby needs new shoes.

All this pondering reminded me of a beach trip my extended family took a few years back. After several hours on the road heading south, our caravan pulled into a fast-food joint to grab some lunch and visit the facilities. The younger kids whined about the restaurant choice. The toys were better at the joint across the street. The teens rolled their eyes at the rest of us, and I had already begun feeling the road grunge that only goes away after a long shower.

At the counter, my older brother, Big G, proceeded to special order for all his family. One child didn't want cheese, another didn't want onions but wanted extra pickles, etc. The order irritated my younger brother, James, to no end. "Never order anything but a No. 1 or a No. 2," he muttered to Big G. "They'll *#% it up every time. Just scrape off the onions."

Yep. This was gonna be a long trip.

Overhearing his comment, the server took offense. "Don't misunderestimate me," said the pimpled Norm Crosby. His name tag read, "Genesis Jones."

"Genesis," my dad said, blue eyes twinkling, "I should start, 'In the beginning,' but I think I'll skip to No. 3." The teenager looked at him blankly. Something tells me we didn't mis-underestimate him.

The rest of us followed James' advice and called out a number. Then we all sat down and waited for our order numbers – not to be confused with our meal numbers – to be called. We had been waiting about 10 minutes when Genesis motioned Big G up to the counter to clarify some confusion on his special order. Was it pickles and no onions, or onions and no pickles? "Just make it five No. 1's," Big G said through gritted teeth.

After another 10 minutes of starvation, Daddy looked around the place and stated dryly, "This would make a great location for a fast-food restaurant." No twinkles, this time.

Which is why I don't understand why Mickey D's would mess with their numbers. I mean, even two year olds know what No. 1 and No. 2 are. Imagine their confusion if you changed them midstream, so to speak.

Surely we all have a fast-food nightmare story, clown or no clown. But we keep goin' back, back, back for more, more, more. Lord know, I'm guilty -- nobody does Diet Coke like Mickey D's.

Sigh. If only I could order a fresh fried hot apple pie to go with it....

Words Fit for the Litter Box

If you're a Southern woman who's ever drawled down your nose at someone of less-refined breeding, as in "Bless her heart. She cleans up pretty good for a Parnell," then you could be accused of being catty.

In studying on this tendency to equate persnickety females with felines, I had an epiphany of sorts.

Like the cat-worshipping Egyptians of antiquity, we mimic what we adore. Just look at the recent comeback of dramatic eye-liner.

I further mused that we not only try to look like cats, but we also talk their talk. In fact, I assert that we stole much of our language from them. So with apologies to Merriam-Webster and Latin teachers everywhere, I offer this CATalog of words to back my reckoning:

The Pursuit of Purr-fection **
A CATalog of terms and definitions related to our feline friends

Cat-a-clys-mic – relating to a violent natural event, as when mice become meals
Cat-a-ma-ran – a boat in which cats can travel dry in water
Cat-as-tro-phe – a cat disaster, such as spilled milk
Cat-a-ton-ic – the mental state of a cat after taking a nip of gin and tonic

Cat-chup – a sauce for spicing up cataclysmic meals

Cat-e-go-ries – a list of registered cat breeds

Cat-er-waul – a shrill howling noise made by cats

Cat-o-nine-tails – a genetic aberration

Cat-ti-tude – self-explanatory

Cat-walk – runway at a pedigree cat show

Hy-purr-bo-le – A cat's big fish tale

Im-purr-fec-tion – all creatures not feline

Kit-ten ca-boo-dle – American cat slang for "baby got back"

Me-ow-ting pot – a country that welcomes immigrant cats and encourages assimilation for breeding Heinz 57 varieties

Me-ow-lo-dra-ma – the screeching exit scene of a skittish cat

Proof of purr-chase – a purebred cat's pedigree papers

Purr-am-e-ter – the distance from which a cat's purr can be heard

Purrch – a high place to sit for a cat's-eye view

Purr-chase pow-er – the extent to which a cat can charm its owner to buy it treats at a pet store

Purr-form – not a word. Cats don't do tricks for people

Purr-fume – the smell of a purrmanent marker (see below)

Purr-loin – a cat's action in stealing a pork loin set out to thaw on a kitchen counter

Purr-ma-nent mar-ker – a male cat's spray in defining his territory; alternate definition: a dead cat's gravestone

Purr-ma-nent wave – a cat's cowlick

Purr-mis-sion – the gracious consent of a cat to be spoiled

Purr-mom-e-ter – A measure of a cat's contentment

Purr-of-the-mo-ment – a cat's spontaneous burst of contentment

Purr-pose – I purr, therefore I am

Purr-snick-et-y – condescending attitude natural to a cat. See also: **Cattitude**

Purr-son-al-i-ty – a cat's temperament. See also: **Cattitude** and **Purrsnickety**

Purr-suit of hap-pi-ness – the inalienable right of a cat to do whatever it darn well pleases

Purr-us-al – a cat's quick scan of its environment to determine interest

** Out of pure laziness at this proof-of-concept stage, and in catlike fashion of doing what I darn well please, I've declined to provide pronunciations – making the broad assumption that if you're still reading for pleasure, you are somewhat familiar with and inclined towards the written word.

And if catty describes you, this CATalog should be an invaluable reference for future sassy asides. Furthermore, if you truly can't say something nice about someone, please join me in the litter box -- where the poop is always fresh and ready to dish.

Listing Through Life with an Unbalanced Load

If there were possibly one word to describe both Fred and me, polar opposites in how we function best, it would be "lister." I know I'm coining a word, so grammarians, chill out. I'll explain.

Fred is organized, on time, prepared and always makes a list before going anywhere or doing anything that requires more than a single point of focus. He is one of those incredibly important people to include on any project (especially a marriage) that you want to succeed.

Case in point – It dawned on me recently that if Fred leaves this life before I do, I have no idea what the combination to the safe is, much less a good understanding of how to access all the insurance policies, etc. So, I asked him to put together a folder for me. Fred loves folders. I love delegation. I'm a big-picture kind of gal.

As God is my witness, when I glanced the next morning at his latest to-do list, I read at the very top (under the date, of course):

Make list for Aunt Sister on safe, etc.

He made a list about making a list. But bless his heart, Fred keeps me in the road. Literally. You see, I'm a lister of a whole 'nother sort. I list when I walk.

I can't go for a stroll with Fred without walking sideways into him. No matter which side I'm on, there's the potential for a collision. After 20 years of marriage, Fred has become adept at moving out of the way, putting on his sneaker brakes so that I shoot past him, or grabbing my shoulders and redirecting my compass.

My frequent consultant, Merriam-Webster, gives definition to this meaning of list, as an intransitive verb: "to tilt to one side; especially of a boat or ship: to tilt to one side in a state of equilibrium (as from an unbalanced load)." I'm sure a few friends and acquaintances would attest to the possibility that my load is unbalanced, but it's the South. We love our oddballs.

I define being a lister as viewing the world a little off center, and behaving accordingly. My diagonal walking is just one symptom.

I come from a long line of listers, including my dear father. For example, Daddy sets his microwave timer at 3:01 instead of 3:00 minutes because, "I don't want to wear out the round numbers."

Little Darlin' is the youngest in our current line of listers. A fond illustration: One day when LD was in first grade, Fred was about to take her and Golden Boy to school. As they were backing out of the driveway, LD realized she had left her homework in the house.

Fred pulled up to let her run in and get it while he and GB sat in the car. After a few minutes, three-year-old GB asked, "Where's Wittle Dahwin?" Fred went in the house and found her at the piano practicing her scales. She totally forgot the task at hand. LD doesn't make lists.

It should come as no surprise that LD, Daddy and I have all made our living as writers. People pay us for that view from a-kilter. Go figure. We also are chronic optimists – dreaming of better ways – which often means we are windmill tilters. (See tilt, above, in definition of list.)

Another trait we share is a lack of directional sense. Unless the sun is blazing from the east or the west, I will flunk spatial orientation. Fred could tell you what road to take by looking at moss growing on a tree 50 yards away.

I still have trouble telling left from right. When seeking driving directions from Fred, I have been known to ask, "Up or down?" Interpretation: Do I push the blinker (turn signal) up (right) or down (left)? Bless my heart.

For LD and me, GPS is a life saver. I'm not sure about Daddy. His aversion to technology and round numerology (as in an address ending in zero) might make seeking directions from a satellite problematic. And then there is that tendency of men to equate asking directions with emasculation....

One has to wonder about some of the ancestry of our lister gene. Maybe we settled in Alabama because great, great, great Granddaddy Horatio tilted at a windmill and listed to the west when traveling by foot to Georgia. Or maybe he refused to ask for directions at the local Trader Joe's...

"I love you." "You're welcome."

One day, when Golden Boy was just a cotton-topped pudge ball, his chubby legs carried him into the den with an urgency preserved in the human genome solely for survival.

"Mr. Fwed, Mr. Fwed! Hehlppp, Mr. Fwed!" he yelled to his step-dad. The sharp keyring opening of a Co-Cola can held his fat little thumb in a death vise.

"Golden Boy," Fred said with the curiosity of a man not unfamiliar with childhood mishaps. "How in this world did you get your thumb stuck in a Coke can?"

GB looked up at him, his face incredulous and full for the first time with the knowledge that adults, indeed, are dumber than dirt. "It don't matter, Mr. Fwed," he said, exasperated. "Get it out." And there it was. Ecclesiastes 3:2 out of the mouth of a three-year-old.

Bless Fred's heart. Without further analysis, he extracted the opposable digit from its snare and wrapped it in a Ninja Turtles Band-Aid.

For the past five years, my family has had a time to question, cry, pray and worry after my baby brother was diagnosed with an incurable brain tumor. It also was a time to marvel at the brave, good humor of our sweet James – husband, father, son, brother, deacon, veteran, musician, prankster, business leader and friend to all who knew him.

It was a time to laugh with him and in fine Southern style, to find the humor that is the B-side of the vinyl record called life. His record was a 45-rpm, not a long-playing album. But what a masterpiece of music.

During his final weeks and days, it was a time for us to be humbled and enveloped by the swift currents of love that lapped over us from all directions, depending on the need. Friends, Christian family, doctors and caregivers wrapped our physical and emotional wounds in big Ninja-Turtle Band-Aids.

"Be sure to take something tomorrow," one concerned family friend said to me on the eve of the funeral. A casserole, pound cake and Klonopin are the secret weapons of Southern women in times of crisis.

James' funeral was a time to celebrate a life lived with not an ounce of waste, and an unfolding legacy beyond our current comprehension. Today, it is also a time to thank, en masse and individually, the hundreds of fine souls who have dressed our wounds and continue to carry us forward.

We have mourned enough. Now is a time to remember the man who told teachers when he started high school that he was not kin to either me or our older brother. He was toast either way, he explained later, because teachers then would set the behavior bar too high or too low. I'll not comment on which of us was the subject of either comparison.

Now is the time to remember him, as a young bachelor, bringing a pink baby quilt to the hospital when my daughter was born. The doctors had told me with 100-percent confidence that I was having a boy, so Little Darlin's nursery was punctuated by a wall-paper border of teddy bears piloting bi-planes in infinite circles. That bothered James tremendously.

The baby quilt he chose was hideous. He was not known for his fashion sense. But it swaddled Little Darlin' and warmed my heart. On subsequent birthdays and Christmases, that same young man gifted all his nieces and one nephew with the most obnoxious noise-making toys he could find. A few years later when his babies came along, payback was hell.

As he lost his ability to conjure up the correct responses to questions and comments, it was time to find the sweetness and humor there. "I love you, sweetie," his home caregiver said to him recently upon leaving for the day.

"You're welcome," he answered her. And he was right. We were welcomed to love him. He loved us all.

And, now, sweet baby James, it's time for peace, rest, heaven and smiles. Bless your heart.

Adios Osceola...
and a Rabbit Tale or Two

While he wasn't as famous as Hank Williams' Kaw-Liga, our former knotty-pine neighbor was every bit as wooden and gaudy, and was a splinter in our collective thumb. At least until he disappeared.

The life-sized carving of Osceola, the historic Seminole leader and mascot of Florida State University, began his local sentinel duty after an FSU couple moved onto The Mountain and perched him on their front porch like Santa Claus.

In the midst of more modest concrete critters and the occasional cherub, Osceola gave new meaning to our understanding of yard art. His year-round presence particularly rankled Miss Annie Fanning, the self-appointed fashion police of curb appeal in our neck of the woods.

I have an unapologetic affinity for tasteful lawn décor, and I'm sure my little garden accents were an aggravation to Miss Annie. But I stopped short of featuring patron saints or the tail ends of resin-molded dogs that appear to have their heads sunk below ground, going about the business of bone retrieval.

Miss Annie tolerated all these smaller offenses as her cross to bear. But bless her heart, she just couldn't abide Osceola. "That is the tackiest thing I have evah seen," she'd say over a plastic glass of wine on our side porch. "It just needs to disappear."

Thus, when Osceola went MIA that autumn, no one doubted who dunnit. We just speculated as to how. Miss Annie weighed a mere 90 pounds, even after Thanksgiving lunch, so there had to be an accomplice or two. But no one talked. We were inclined to be glad of Osceola's demise, whether for aesthetic or athletic reasons.

But time passes, and eventually the wooden Native American was just a smoke signal of a memory. Then on Christmas Eve, Miss Annie received a unique anonymous gift. Inside the wrapping was the most pitiful concrete bunny I have ever seen. Sitting up on its haunches, it was missing its two front feet and an ear. Tied around its neck with raffia was a typed note:

Dear Miss Annie,

I come to you on the recommendation of the garden gnomes, with whom I have been hiding the past few months after escaping from my cruel human owners. You have a reputation far and wide, dear, dear Miss Annie, as the Guardian Angel of unwanted yard art, so I am appealing to your generous heart to provide me the permanent sanctuary I so desperately need.

You see, the gnomes will serve only as temporary shelter for species other than their own, and it was time for me to find a new home.

My sob story began five years ago, when my owners bought me at a flea market for $2 after my first owner liquidated and moved. My new owners forced me to sit on top of a 1978 TV console with my twin (we multiply, you know), to hold up a plywood mantle in their doublewide. On top of the plank they stuck the TV's rabbit ears smack dab in front of a velvet painting of the Zodiac signs.

But when lightning blew out the TV, it also sent me flying. In land-ing, I broke the glass top off a wagon wheel coffee table. Taking this as a bad omen, they took a hammer and whacked off my front feet for good-luck charms, one for each of them. Then the man, reeking of Ripple, picked me up by my ears to put me back on the TV and broke my left ear clean off. In a rage, he threw me out in the rain until he sobered up. Then his practical side took over and he retrieved me, put me in the bathroom and used my good ear as a toilet paper holder.

When they emptied the trailer for spring hosing down, I finally made a run to the underground network of mistreated yard art, and the gnomes took me in. When it was time for me to go, they wrapped me up and delivered me to you, Miss Annie, knowing that you would do right by me.

Please, please help.

> *Your friend,*
> *Lucky the Rabbit*

Miss Annie, through tears of laughter, took in Lucky and stored him, I'm sure, in a warm, dry basement corner. Icicle stalactites would form on the roof of hell before that poor maimed creature would find the light of day in her yard.

Around Easter, though, Lucky showed up with a big purple bow around his neck in our front yard – 60 miles away from The Mountain – and two dozen little plastic bunnies lined up in for-mation behind him.

"Guess what?" read the note around his neck. "Lucky is a girl."

They multiply, you know.

Lock, Stock and Murphy

"That's just Murphy. He must be off his meds."

That was our first sign of storm clouds ahead. It couldn't have been clearer if a tornado-born bobble head of James Spann the Weather Man had cold-cocked our noggins.

But did Fred or I listen? Let's just say we chose not to hear.

We were buying our first lake place – a 900-square-foot cinder-block dugout on a remote island off an Alabama lake tributary, accessible by land only by a three-mile red-dirt road.

You knew the asphalt was about to end when you passed a 1955 rusted-out Ford Fairlane planted on the left shoulder. It had squatter's rights that no one questioned, and was now home to generations of privet, muscadine vines and serpents of Eden.

The property's flaws were many – too remote, no water filtration system, rotting boat house and more. Let's just say we chose not to see.

We tunnel-visioned on the view, which was worthy of a Field and Stream cover. To us, it was paradise.

At the closing table with the sellers, Mr. and Mrs. Porter, we learned that the deal had to be delayed because a crazy man had run the surveyor off. The surveyor was going back the next day escorted by a sheriff's deputy.

Downplaying any resemblance to a Stephen King setting, Mrs. Porter clued us in on the nutcase. Murphy was to be our next-door neighbor.

"He's harmless," she said.

Murphy was a 40-ish-year-old man whose parents had moved him to the lake and then conveniently passed away. A legal guardian of some sort managed his affairs from afar.

Although never confirmed – and certainly none of my business – I presumed that Murphy was schizophrenic. Whatever his ailment, he came with the deal. The Porters had built the place 25 years before we bought it, and he had done them no harm. They were such nice old folks, so we took them at their word. Bless our hearts.

That little island was a Pandora's Box of quirky characters: a chain-smoking red-neck millionaire couple whose boat house sheltered every conceivable water toy money could buy, and whose driveway was marked by concrete gargoyles with red-painted eyes; a man who shared his cabin with 30-plus wild cats until neighbors pressed the law to intervene; Murphy; and, of course, us.

Murphy usually kept to himself, unless he got a hankering to leave the island. Dressed in a preppy button-down, shorts and loafers, hair combed neatly, he looked perfectly sane as he climbed into his brown pickup truck. But when he peeled out, going from zero to 60 in 10 seconds, he left a couple of flattened cats and a host of cursing neighbors in his dusty wake. He sometimes yelled back at them with quite imaginative insults. He never uttered a word to me.

Murphy spent most days working on his rip wall – a rock border along his expansive shoreline. Cold Creek Rock jutted up like a giant shark fin across the inlet from his property at the island's point, taunting him with its graffiti and the raucous activities of circling swimmers. The Rock was a favorite diving site for teenagers and Darwinian adults -- "Hold my beer and watch this," being the preamble to most leaps.

Altercations between the drunks and the disturbed echoed off the pine-covered hills on the other side of Cold Creek. One day we heard Murphy call an attractive young woman a "milk cow," and then proceed to tell her she had "the morals of a goat." I rechecked the bolt on our door.

But Murphy was better than a guard dog for us, given our infrequent presence. He never trespassed, getting worked up only when strangers stepped foot on or swam near his land or ours.

So when we decided to sell the place a few years later, we almost chose not to mention Murphy. Almost. The buyers were kinfolk by marriage, so we felt a bit obliged to clue them in.

"He's harmless, even when he's off his meds," Fred said. And that was that. The couple chose to buy it anyway – lock, stock and Murphy.

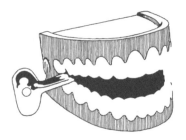

On Teeth, T-Ledgers and Smelly Reputations

True confession. I mainline Dear Abby like my 15-year-old nephew snarfs deviled eggs at a family reunion. When the letters are good, there's nothing better. Except perhaps, a good obituary.

Case in point -- a couple of weeks ago, I read this gem:

"Dear Abby:

A friend of mine died recently. My question is, how much time should I wait before asking his widow if she saved his hearing aids from the crematorium, and if so, could I have them?

CHEAP MINNESOTAN"

Where do these people come from? Oh, right. Minnesota.

The kicker was that Abby advised him to be respectful, but not to wait too long, or someone else would beat him to the punch.

While I question the question, the advice was spot on. When I did a little research, I found that there is quite a market for used hearing aids, as people "trade up" on models or, like the friend of our Minnesota writer, leave this world and their hearing needs behind.

This should come as some comfort to my dad, who weighs every dollar spent on quality-of-life enhancements against their potential return on investment. A few years ago, he balked at getting dentures after projecting their cost per annum over 10 years. His planning assumption was that he wouldn't live longer than his father had.

Mother told him she didn't care if he dropped dead next week, she wasn't going to be married to a character out of Deliverance. Daddy invested. He now has outlived his own forecast by quite a stretch.

Then, there is the time-value of "get-ups." You see, Daddy figures he has only five good "get-ups" a day, discounting health and hygiene. For him to get up out of his leather navy recliner and turn off John Wayne, it's got to be pretty darn important. I'm proud to say that I rate a get-up every time I visit. Oh course, I do live out of town.

I find myself making similar calculations when faced with climbing the stairs to the second floor of our house. Light bulb packs, clean towels and toilet paper will balance for days like Jenga blocks on the bottom-stair bannister before I get motivated enough to make the trek.

Fred and I are empty nesting now, so wasting knee joints on the upkeep of second-floor bedrooms is not high on our agenda. Usually, the tipping point has to do with the impending arrival of guests. The dogs really don't care.

Another recent Dear Abby that made my morning coffee backflow went like this:

"Dear Abby,

"I am a girl in my junior year in high school. My boyfriend of three years is very good to me, affectionate, attentive and very good looking. I don't think he cheats on me, but he does have serious flatulence. ..."

Bless her heart.

This young lady has quite a dilemma. Maybe a T-chart with pros on one side and cons on the other would be helpful. In this situation I'd give far more negative weight to the one big con on the boyfriend's ledger, especially in light of her resounding endorsement of his fidelity.

I don't remember what words of wisdom Abby imparted, but I'm with Mother on this one. My advice: "Honey, don't ever tie your reputation to a character out of Deliverance. It's just, well, common. Dump him now."

Decisions to invest in a smile or divest of a smell are really no decisions at all. The avoided cost is social bankruptcy.

Send-Offs with a Six-Pack

"Where's Granddaddy?' my kids asked many a day after barreling into my parents' house looking for their afternoon sitter. "Oh, he's gone totin'," Mother would answer. "He'll be back in a bit."

Daddy toted about as often as he went to the barber or stopped by the Pig (Piggly Wiggly) for milk. Satisfied with the routine answer, Little Darlin' and Golden Boy would get out their blocks and wait for his return. They had no clue he was putting a body in the ground.

You see, on The Mountain where I'm from, we take care of our own, cradle to grave. But sometimes that requires a little help from strangers. Enter the enterprising Right Rev. James A. Mootauchy, Jr, our retired pastor.

Brother Jim, as we call him, created a cottage industry to help mortuaries give a proper send-off to dead folks who don't have enough friends and family nearby to close the deal. He recognized the opportunity when called on by funeral directors to say a eulogy for departing souls who didn't have a local minister to bid them farewell.

When pallbearers were also needed, mortuaries began outsourcing the service to Brother Jim rather than tying up their own staff. He built up his clientele quickly -- supply and demand being what they are -- and heaven was the limit.

After Daddy retired, Brother Jim enlisted him as one of his pallbearers-on-call. He needed a robust lineup of good backs with respectful countenances to deliver his charges to their post-mortem appointments.

The pallbearers, usually a six-pack, called themselves "toters." In Daddy's time, a toter would make $30 to $40 a haul, depending on time and walking distance involved. A $30 "tote-and-drop" covered a reasonable walk from hearse to grave, where Brother Jim delivered a few final words.

But occasionally, when funeral attendees were so few as to be unseemly, "we were asked to sit in on the service to make it look like somebody was there," Daddy said. That garnered the extra sawbuck.

On one $40 engagement, the toters were asked to sit front and center during a long Greek Orthodox funeral and were almost overwhelmed by the incense released right under their Baptist noses.

Daddy told me the usual "totee" was:
- A native of The Mountain who had moved away years earlier and then was returned for burial;
- A local who had out-lived friends and who had few, if any, surviving relatives;
- One whose family was well-heeled and would rather pay someone than impose on people; and/or
- A family renegade whose kin wanted things done as quickly and as anonymously as possible.

Bless their hearts.

Now toting wasn't just a walk in the, umm, park. Professional pallbearers had to be careful not to trip in low places, step in mud or trounce on existing graves. But when they had a lengthy trek ahead -- and no one was around to witness -- "the hearse driver would accommodate us and back right up to the grave," Daddy recalled fondly.

Once, they had a near miss navigating a casket down several concrete church steps to the sidewalk in raw, icy weather. "Almost dropped that one," he said with a tinge of relief.

There was also the inevitable jockeying for position. Each toter vied for the end of the casket holding the legs (it was lighter). In one case, the deceased had lost a leg, making the stakes even higher.

Another time, Daddy's car of three toters got tied up in traffic at the funeral home and lost the cemetery caravan. "We didn't tote because no one knew where the country graveyard was located," he said. "We just drove home, and the other three toters had to draft help."

Before Daddy aged out of toting, he earned enough one year to require filing a W-2 form with the IRS – death and taxes being what they are.

And these universal truths, combined with a good quality service, keep Brother Jim averaging more than one funeral every two days even now. Because on The Mountain, folks take care of our own, cradle to grave.

Goulash, Goldfish and Cocky Little Girls

I used to think Mother was the world's best at stretching a meal when money was tight. We loved her "goulash," concocted from a little hamburger meat, a handful of elbow macaroni and a lot of tomato sauce. But she had nothing on the Master.

Last Sunday our pastor preached an inspired message on John 6:1-14, which details how Jesus turned five loaves and two fish into more food than you can get on a West Alabama catfish farm. Five thousand fed, with leftovers to boot.

The pew warmers chuckled as Pastor Ray pulled out one plastic bag holding a few little Goldfish crackers and another stuffed with five hamburger buns. You gotta give a man his props on props. We got the point. This miracle was, in Trump-speak, a BIG DEAL. HUGE. As he transitioned into the greater meaning of spiritual hunger fed by the Bread of Life, my thoughts went back to the early 1970s and that goulash.

Mother dished it up after the Sunday night service when our children's choir performed "The Boy Who Caught the Fish," a cantata based on the same scripture Pastor Ray spoke to. I'll never forget it – I played The Boy. Bless my heart.

This was not a gender-bender situation in which bathroom usage at the Baptist church was at stake. I got the part either because none of the boys would do it, or because they couldn't carry a tune. I never really knew. It didn't matter. The boys' voices had not changed, and neither had the girls' chests. A ponytail and a head cover did the trick.

Barefoot, dressed in a white tunic draped with blue cloth and cinched with a sash, I held my fishing-pole prop like a trophy. When the time came for my big solo, I stood front-and-center, my legs in Superman stance, and belted out:

"Yeah, yeah, I caught a fi-ish
"Yeah, yeah, I caught another ....

(insert several stanzas)

"And THAT MAKES ME a BET-ter FISH-er-MAN than any other. YEAH!"

That Boy was a cocky little so-and-so, at least until he got religion a few songs later and learned to share. Kudos to Jack Coleman, who in 1972 wrote something kids could hum to and remember 45 years later. Indeed, it played over and over in my head ad nauseam once the memory neuron fired last week.

But it also reminded me how earnest kids are and how important EVERYTHING is when you're little. And, how grateful I am that our parents hauled our little fannies to church every time the doors opened.

Church choir was part heaven and part sheer hell. When we were learning a cantata, our minister of music, Mr. Billhurn, reverently handed out the numbered sheet music (no copies allowed -- copyright being very important to the music industry and honesty important to the church).

He dropped the record-player needle on whatever song we were trying to memorize. We sang along happily, pleased with the full, melodious sounds we thought we were producing. After a few rounds of fun, he took us cold turkey from the professionally produced album to never-ending sectional drills while we learned our parts.

Our accompanist, Mr. Billhurn's teenaged daughter Carrie, pinged out the notes of each part over and over as the 9-to-11-year-olds in that voice section sang along. All of us made a joyful noise, some even on tune. Then we went to the next part. And the next.

By show time, we all knew our parts and attacked them with zeal. At least the kids who didn't get stage fright looking out at the pew warmers. There were no cell-phone photos snapped, but there were plenty of proud parents grinning ear-to-ear.

Mr. Billhurn taught us a lot about treble clefs; bass clefs; quarter-, half- and whole-notes; and that hard work pays off. I'm sure cuteness held sway over talent in our performance, but we didn't know that then. We were cocky little so-and-sos, especially when Mother rewarded us with lavish reviews and bowls of goulash, Goldfish crackers swimming on top.

A Marriage on the Gridiron

Pretzel-Throwing Season is officially upon us. Before the first kick-off of the college football season, many Southeastern Conference fans break out the cold beer, hot wings, redneck caviar and corn chips. In our house, Fred breaks out the pretzel bag, and I break out the Dirt Devil.

This tradition started the fall after we married 20 years ago. During a tight game that mattered more to most Southern men than their daughter's honor, Fred's team choked on a play. Next thing I knew, the pretzel poised for Fred's mouth was sent hurling to a new receiver – the TV.

"Are you finished?" I asked, amused. Scratch the notion that women tend to emote more than men. At least not around here, on game days.

Goal posts have framed our relationship from the start. For one of our first dates, Fred snagged two decent tickets to the Alabama/Tennessee game, back when we played in the old Iron Lady, Legion Field, in Birmingham. This also was in the days before most games were televised. For someone who didn't have season tickets, Fred had done good.

We were sitting about a third of the way up from the field on the 35-yard line. "How do you like these seats?" Fred asked me, his chest puffing out.

"I don't know," I answered honestly. "I've never sat in the stands before." Fred's chest caved in like Aunt Vernie's sweet potato soufflé, pulled out of the oven in the 100-percent humidity of an Alabama August. If Fred had had a pretzel, he'd have thrown it. Bless his heart.

I was totally insensitive to my insensitivity. I was just telling the truth. When I went to games as a kid, I was my dad's guest in the press box. He was an AP reporter, and on throw-away games, he would rotate his extra seat between my brothers and me. The only rule, which he drilled in before every game, was that we couldn't cheer for either team, or we'd be ejected. So I learned early to sit quietly, watch and help keep statistics.

During football season in those days, we ate our Sunday dinners on TV trays while Dad covered the Bear Bryant and Shug Jordan shows, capturing day-after comments from the legendary coaches on his portable, manual typewriter. He deftly turned them into wire copy, which he then dictated over the phone for Monday papers across the nation.

We sat quietly while he worked, or we'd be ejected. There was no rewind on that black-and-white TV. So through no particular interest on my part, I drank in football strategy much like we shared a Coke with the Bear.

Fred didn't know my family history when we went to that first game together. But his chest soon recovered from the ego blow as we got into the game. After a four-and-out series, Bama punted and backed Tennessee up to the 11-yard line. "At least we have field position," I remarked off-handedly.

"You know what field position is?" Fred asked. The cartoon hearts ding-dinged in his eyes like a two-columned slot machine jackpot. Bingo! He gave me a ring that November.

On New Year's Day, the Rev. Dr. James A. Mootauchy married us at 9 a.m., with my parents, brother James and his wife as witnesses. After a small reception at James' house, we settled in to watch Bama play in the Liberty Bowl. Pretzel-Throwing Season was upon us.

Now, two decades later, I sit by (somewhat) quietly during football games, old habits being what they are. But I am poised for action with the Dirt Devil by my side.

At least I have field position.

Wearing the Sling of Outrageous Fortune

Safe in the sanctuary of her evergreen walls, Fauna is laughing at me with all the sympathy of the sprite she is. Fauna lives in our parterre because I dreamed a dream and was too cheap to write a check.

Parterre is a fancy French word for a formal garden of hedge-lined gravel paths. I have one. Not to put on airs, mind you, but to hide an eyesore.

Our home's previous owners had dug out a chunk of the back-yard and filled it with chert. Chert is a fancy word for fine gravel. The chert bed was the base for a wooden play structure that the family took with them when they moved. Hence the eyesore.

Grass won't grow over a foot of gravel, so I filled the square with bird feeders. It quickly sprouted a layer of seed hulls, weeds and other avian deposits.

My cousin James Farmer, a landscape designer, suggested a par-terre. When I figured out what the heck it was, I decided to go for it. But James lives in Georgia, and Fred was not into fancy garden rooms.

I was on my own, and went about my project with the gusto of the dumb fool that I was. Bless my heart. I hired a retired extension agent to excavate enough for the boxwood rows and to dig a three-foot-square hole in the center for a water feature. Water feature is a fancy term for fountain.

James had taught me a few years back how to build rock walls, and I had employed this skill in the past to elevate flower beds and impress the neighbors.

So after the backhoe work was done, I dismissed the paid labor. "I got this," I told myself.

And I did. When I was done, I proudly surveyed the stacked-stone border wall behind the garden, and the plastic-lined fountain bed nestled inside an 18-inch-tall rock wall supported by cinderblocks that I had installed and plumbed level.

Fred and Golden Boy looked on amused, and went back into the air conditioning to watch NASCAR.

I laid down granite slabs to form pathways; and then added soil to the border ruts, where I planted 40 small Japanese boxwoods that would fill in to form hedges. I hauled in bags of larger gravel, which I spread between the pavers, and planted a weeping fig tree in the back corner for a nice accent.

The garden was now ready for Fauna, a bronze wood nymph fountain I had ordered from a catalog. I placed Fauna on a pedestal in the water feature, carved fig leaves covering the top of her head and other strategic places. Standing on tiptoe, she smiled sweetly at me and stretched her arms down to feel the water splash through her fingertips. I smiled back.

As I write this on my patio years later, Fauna has acquired a little patina that has gone to her head. She now grins at me with the air of a Shakespearian imp. But she is not Puck, and the stuff of my dreams are not of a Midsummer's Night.

I am starring in my own little nightmare called a detached supraspinatus tendon, which is a fancy term for torn rotator cuff, and this is its encore presentation.

The doctor says it's from wear and tear, not one big injury. I guess I built one rock wall too many. With medical bills past and pending, my little parterre is now a very expensive Parterre.

Because, if I'm going to wear a sling and suffer for my art, it's going to have a highfalutin' name.

Faceless Voices and Things that Go 'Garrump' in the Night

Fred and I recently hosted a reception for some New York consultants in town to help out a non-profit. The two women were well-educated, sophisticated urbanites in all-black dresses and slick-backed hair. As we stood on our deck having evening cocktails, the resident frogs from the creek below began their nightly garrumps.

"Are those deer?" one of our guests asked. Bless her heart.

Discounting road rage incidents and Black Friday shopping mall free-for-alls, close encounters with strangers can be among the funniest or touching of experiences.

For instance, Little Darlin', who fractured her ankle last month, was hobbling on crutches down a long hallway in the hospital where she works. A patient in a wheelchair came up from behind her, lifted his sunglasses to catch her eyes, and – as he left her in his dust – said, "Vroom! Vroom!"

You just can't make this stuff up.

My friend Bets and I still get tickled remembering a trip to New Orleans a few years ago. We had been shopping for quite a while, and I was pooped. At our last stop, as we were trying on clothes in adjoining dressing room stalls, I told her I was ready to call it quits.

Disappointed, she replied loudly, "What? No Saks this afternoon?"

Startled for a few seconds, I finally understood. "Oh, I thought you said 'no sex this afternoon!'" I commented back.

"So did I," called out a faceless voice. We all laughed, and the stranger exited before we ever got a glimpse of her.

Then, there is Fred's lovely custom of doing random acts of kindness. One day he bought the meal of the woman behind him in the drive-thru of a local restaurant. Waving, he drove off and floated for days on the high of good works.

The next time he needed his do-gooder fix, he visited the same drive-thru and repeated the drill. When he waved to the lucky recipient, he realized it was the same woman he had gifted the last time.

"She is going to report you as a stalker," I told him when he relayed the story to me. It's easy to put a worry hex on Fred.

My favorite strange encounter occurred about a year ago. I was about to enter an office building to see a friend, and I held the door open for three women exiting. The third one was a pixie with a blond-bob haircut. She honed in on the turquoise ring I wore on my right hand, smiled, and in a clipped British accent that outpaced my Alabama ears, she talked excitedly, pointed to my ring, and then pointed to the smaller turquoise ring she wore.

She took hers off and handed it to me to try on. I said it wouldn't fit, but she told me to put it on my pinky. So I did. She smiled again and started to walk away, leaving her ring behind. "Wait," I said, touched by her gesture. I took off my own ring and gave it to her to try on. It fit her middle finger, albeit loosely. Then she started to take it off to return it. "Keep it," I said.

"Really?" she asked. "I give people things all the time, and no one has ever given something back to me." She grinned and skipped on out.

I relayed the exchange to my friend. "You know the good doctor's office is down the hall," he said.

But I didn't care whether or not my ring buddy was a bit "tetched" in the head. She had given me a gift of self that brightens my day every time I sport my new ring. I hope she feels the same.

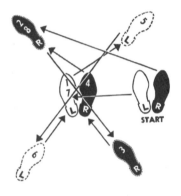

The Big Bird Cha-Cha and the Commando Waltz

When my gut does the backflips my other body parts could never master, I should listen. Always. I have a tangerine tutu and nightmares to remind me.

A few years ago, I had the "opportunity" to be a star in a local charity version of Dancing with the Stars. I was uneasy about committing, given my lack of adequate practice time and limb coordination. But my dear friend Gina Marie had ponied up the year before, waltzing elegantly to "Unchained Melody" with her pro dancing partner. So I took one for the team and agreed to cha-cha for charity.

What I failed to factor in was Gina Marie's head cheerleader pedigree. That was back in the day when high school cheerleaders built human pyramids, three-perky-people high; threw their hands up to enliven a bleacher full of disaffected pouty teenagers; and through fixed, million-dollar smiles, pleaded, "Y'all ye-yahl." (For you Yankees, that loosely rhymes with, "All Hail.") The "flyers" then dismounted in backflips followed by handsprings.

Gina Marie was a flyer. I took art.

But I convinced myself that "One, two, cha-cha-cha," couldn't be too hard, especially keeping time with the moderately paced song I had chosen. I figured I would get in a couple hours' practice a week, wear a stunning royal blue or red dress to the event, and muck my way through it with a cheerleader smile and good humor.

But when I met my partner, the good humor bar melted down my wrist and fell plop on the sidewalk. These people were serious! My partner and his wife competed all over the South, and he was in it to win it. As for the other novices, at least one man hired a personal trainer to decrease his waistline and increase his stamina. Some were practicing three hours a day, five days a week, for months. With my job, I was lucky to be in town that much in a two-week stretch.

Our volunteer choreographer nixed my choice of music. We have to speed it up and make it sizzle, she said. She selected Jennifer Lopez' insanely fast and upbeat "Let's Get Loud" for my bit. I had never met the instructor before, so I have no clue why she hated me so much. Then I told her I was going to wear red. "Red's taken," she said curtly. So were royal blue, teal, white, etc. I didn't know there could only be one of each color. It was a charity event, for Pete's sake. My color assignment was tangerine orange. Just peel me now.

It took some internet searching worthy of a treasure hunt to find an orange tango dress that fully covered major body parts and had enough billowy skirt to get that swish thing right.

A week before the big event, we performed our piece for the instructor's review. "It needs a big wow factor," she said. "Slide under his legs and let him swoop you back up to your feet." My go-to-hell look must have bitch-slapped her back to reality, and we settled for a less ambitious flourish I might could handle if I held my tongue just so.

Come Dance Day, our little community was abuzz with latent talent ready to spring forward for a cause. I had my jitters in check until I debuted my tangerine-spangled, feather-accented designer masterpiece for Fred, my parents and my friend Shannon, who had come down from Nashville to cheer me on. "My Lord, Sister, you look just like Big Bird with a bouffant," she said. Don't you just love friends who lift you up on the wings of eagles? Love you, too, Shannon. Get out of my face.

Anyway, when D-Day hour approached and our names were called, my partner and I cha-cha'd bravely across the stage and back, dipping, twirling and managing to remember and execute the routine with no major big orange crush splattered on the floor.

Two of the judges were generous, playing their celebrity roles in good fun. The third, wouldn't you know it, was a purist. "You moved your feet wrong in that one step," he told me. "I seen it. I seen it." I guess he spent more time in dance class than in English class.

"Ya'll ye-yahl," I silently begged the audience through false eyelashes and gritted teeth, smiling in the face of utter social ruin. Thankfully, clapping, whistles and a couple of cat calls validated that I had at least a few friends or sympathizers in my corner.

Gina Marie couldn't attend that evening. I think sock washing was involved. When I later described it to her, she finally 'fessed up about her night in the spotlight. While backstage with the other dancers awaiting the opening curtain, Gina Marie caught an image of herself in a mirror and saw that the backlight was shining right through her beautiful sheer white chiffon, causing her unmentionables to glow in full glory.

Summoning the crisis-management skills she had developed over a long corporate career, she quickly and discreetly ditched the offending garment and flowed gracefully through her waltz like Anna and the King of Siam. "It wasn't like I could borrow someone's underwear," she recalled with chagrin.

The week before her performance, Gina Marie's instructor had added a few twists to her routine, just as she did with mine. Must be part of the hazing ritual. But Gina Marie nailed her high kicks and a "wipe-out" slide across the floor as only a former head cheerleader could do. "You really know how to place a kick," one judge told her generously. His smile twinkled. What kind of commando show did she give him? She still wonders, bless her heart.

Talking Turkey about the Left Wing

This month, I discovered a special empathy for Tom Turkey when I went under the carving knife myself. Basted in antiseptic and stuffed with saline solution from a drip, I was a regular Butter Ball (no wisecracks, please), and my left shoulder was the drumstick.

Pre-op prep included showering with "chlorhexidine gluconate 4 percent solution" three nights running, and changing the bed sheets before retiring the first night. No pets and no Fred allowed near the bed once the germ warfare began. Bless Fred's heart. Labeled unclean and gone to the dogs.

Perfectly sanitized and ready to get this thing done, I was downright cheery when the admitting nurse processed this turkey. I admit it was a bit Pollyanna-ish, given that this was a do-over repair.

I knew from the previous procedure that it was nothing compared to the physical therapy that would follow. But as Old Man Prater told Fred years ago after quitting Wild Turkey cold turkey, "You know it's time to change your ways when the bad feels worse than the good feels good."

Okay, it's not a perfect analogy. There's no good feeling when you've got a bad wing. But I knew the short-term torture of rehab would be better than spending the rest of my life as if county wrasslin' champ Big Beau LaBelle had wrenched out my arm. I never did like Beauregard, even if he is my cousin. His eyes habitually roll half-shut when he talks.

The intake nurse verified my name, date of birth, surgeon, type of surgery and – most importantly – which shoulder, then snapped a blue plastic band on my right arm and sent me on down the line.

Once I was gowned and on the bed, the next nurse asked again for name, DOB and clarity on which limb was at stake. "LEFT arm," I said. Then the anesthesiologist asked again. I calmly answered, but I was getting a little irritated that these people were so unsure of where they were carving.

Then came the surgeon, who verified again, and inked some kind of Chinese mark on my left shoulder that I thought would settle the question once and for all. I did find comfort that he asked.

Another nurse slipped into the curtained "room" to insert my intravenous drip, and -- you guessed it – she was as curious as the rest about what exactly they were going to do. Now I was just downright annoyed with the whole risk-management protocol. Lawyers run the world.

The IV nurse was chattering away about a roommate who moved out and stuck her with their power bill as she stuck my right wrist with a mile-long needle.

My revenge on the lawyers was swift. I immediately started to faint, eye-lids trying to close, skin breaking into a clammy sweat and chest panting like a thirsty dog. "I'm sorry, sweetie," the nurse said, realizing for the first time that I was in the room. "Wiggle your toes."

Wiggle your own toes, I thought, as they tried to calm me. Six nurses swarmed in and went to work. Fred was again banished from the bedside. Cold towels on my neck and face followed, and I slowly calmed down and started breathing normally.

By then, they were wheeling me down the hall past a host of nurses, residents and mildly curious technicians. "Had a little vena vagal, did you?" one charming young intern chirped. I cut him a look that would have struck him dead if my half-shut rolling eyes could kill.

Then it was all over. I woke up with my right – as in correct – arm in a sling and ready to face the physical therapy to come. At least I have my Wild Turkey. Tom gets a pardon this year, bless his heart.

Mirror Time or Mullet Tossing?

Thanks to his new underwear, Fred thinks he will be adding weeks, if not years, to his free time.

With apologies to T. S. Eliot, whose depressing protagonist J. Alfred Prufrock measured out his life with coffee spoons, Fred has a new, umm, yardstick by which to measure time.

Advocates of this miracle underwear claim its unique patented access system frees up to 217 minutes a year in avoided personal potty time. Fred drank their Kool-Aid. In fact, he was so excited by his new boxer briefs and the comfort and free time that come with them, that he gifted Golden Boy with a couple of pairs. Given GB's youth, he may even accumulate up to nine days in comp time if he has no assisted-living issues for the next 60 years.

Fred's savings, conservatively, should be about three days max, bless his heart. But three days is three days! That's an extra golf tournament, three extra days of college football – or better yet – three days with a fishing pole and a lawn chair.

My usually analytical husband couldn't answer my questions on how the manufacturers did their cyphering. He just took their word. I had to wonder how they figured in differences in age and frequency of activities associated with the time savings. My accountant friends would probably say they normalized the data based on some actuarial tables. Whatever. And then there is the resounding endorsement of that great American Howard Stern. As I said, whatever.

All I know is that if we girls figured out how to save just one minute in our morning beauty routines, we could travel the globe and back in all that spare time. I may even start a campaign.

For those of us 50-somethings with a certain Southern grace to maintain, I'm assuming we've got about 30 more years of daily glamming. Throwing out leap-year variations to keep from over-complicating things, a one-minute-a-day savings would give us a good seven days in the end. Not quite enough time to trot the globe, but a whole week in the Redneck Riviera would allow plenty of time for sun worshipping, mullet tossing and outlet mall shopping.

And you 20-something darlings, listen up. By this same calculation, based on 60 more years of primping, you'll accumulate a whopping 15 days! That's a lot of coffee spoons, sisters… Might even be a quick trip to France and some serious shopping time.

But who's kidding whom? If I decide to really get serious with my time-savings campaign, I probably won't focus on mirror time. Even an extra week isn't worth rushing through a routine that improves both my appearance and my disposition. Did you ever try to rush a Southern Lady? Fred gave up years ago. He just focuses on controlling things over which he has eminent domain, like his personal potty time.

I think a more lucrative endeavor for me would be to bottle the time I spend fretting over things I can't change. Things that come to mind are the weather, the amount of trash under a teenager's bed – assuming ants aren't in the picture – and the aging effects of time itself.

Then there is the time spent trying to figure out how to save something that can't be banked in the first place. Even if we could get an extra week at the beach when we're 85, we'd probably be too worried about the heat to enjoy it. And then, there are the associated wrinkles. Bless our hearts, and pass the coffee spoons. Time's a-wasting.

Dusting for Paw Prints

"Don't look at me with mournful eyes," my mother recently told Little Darlin's begging Shih Tzu, Judy Garland, who was visiting from Atlanta. Mother was drinking a cold beer at the time and saw no need to share the love. "I don't have one thing for you. Mm, hmm. You'd better be backing up."

The love-hate relationship between Mother and our pets is the stuff of family legend. It also sits up and begs to be exploited. That's how a good-natured laugh evolved into a gas-lighting episode in the wag of a tail.

Two points of background:

First, for those readers too wet behind the ears to know what "gas-lighting" means, it's basically an attempt to mess with somebody's head. It originated with a 1938 play, Gas Light, and was made into two movies, the most notable one by George Cukor in 1944. Usually, it means trying to convince someone that his or her perception is not reality, when it really is. In the case of Mom v. Dog, the reality was not her perception. Mind games, regardless.

Second, my mother is not what one might describe as a pet lover. Growing up as she did on a hardscrabble farm, childhood taught her that domesticated animals had functions – they earned their keep. Dogs protected the family and farm. Cats rid it of rodents.

They couldn't do much about resident rats of the human persuasion, like old Cousin Vester. That usually took a party-line call to the county sheriff. "Cousin Vester comes from Silvercross," Mother used to say. "All those Silvercross boys were mean." But, I digress.

In mid-century rural Alabama, pets served as both ADT Home Security and the Orkin Man, and worked for food. They lived outdoors under porches and dined on table scraps or mice. Daddy and Mother largely shared that view, so when we came along, our pets belonged outdoors and knew their place. They could come in on occasion to visit, or to keep warm when it was freezing outside, but those were exceptions.

As adults, my brothers and I have taken a decidedly more pet-friendly bent, especially with our dogs. I'll admit that Mother has softened some with the cajoling of grandkids, but she still doesn't want to be licked, kissed or jumped on by a puppy.

"You are here by invitation only because you are my granddaughter's dog," she told Judy Garland as a follow up to denying her a taste of Miller Lite. Heaven forbid we refer to our pups as "granddogs." Mother does not bestow kinship on strays of any kind (think Cousin Vester) or on four-legged pedigrees.

So imagine her surprise a few years ago, when Angel Grace, the Westie owned by my brother James' family, sent her a Mother's Day card. Upon opening the Hallmark greeting, Mom called me straight away. "Wellll…," she began in her best South-Alabama drawl. "You'll nevah guess who sent me a Mutha's Day card."

I answered with the appropriately curious, "Who?"

"Angel Grace!" she said. "But I know it was Brandon." My nephew Brandon was 10 years old at the time and quite a little devil. Mother went on to conspire with me that she was not going to mention the card. I agreed that was a brilliant strategy. Brandon would either have to wonder forever whether or not it arrived or be the first to blink and 'fess up. Checkmate for Mother.

Problem was, Brandon didn't send it, so he never knew he was suspected.

So, when Angel Grace, in her childish print, sent Mother a birthday card in September, complete with paw print, she called me again with a new theory.

"It was James," she declared, accusing Brandon's dad. "He called to make sure I had gotten the birthday card he sent, but I know he was fishing about that damn dog card. The little shit disguised his handwriting to make it look like Brandon sent it."

Truth was, James had been a little late getting his card in the mail, and he was, indeed, sincerely getting credit for remembering his mother's birthday. He got credit, all right. Bless his heart.

Angel Grace never sent another card, and Mother never mentioned it to James or Brandon, so they never did have the opportunity to deny.

But that Silvercross gene didn't die out with Cousin Vester. Let's just say the postmark from my home 60 miles away from my folks is the same as theirs.

It might be time for the Georgia grand-dog Judy Garland to send Mother a thank you note for the invitation to visit. Next time I'm over that way, I'll mail it for her.

No Signs of Brain Activity

I was sleeping better than your average hibernating bear Friday night when a dog's scream made me and the hairs on my neck jump to attention. That's right. A scream. Not a howl, bark or whine. This freakish cry was infused with panic and pain.

I rushed to the source – our eight-year-old Bichon Frise, Truman – whose lower jaw was wedged into one of the cross-hatched wire grids on the door of his kennel. It took a few minutes for me to pry his teeth loose from their metallic dental floss, and another few for me to calm him down.

He finished the night in our bed, bless his palpitating heart.

As I lay awake dreaming of dreaming again, I couldn't help but think about Truman and wonder, "What was he thinking?" to stick his jaw in the screen. He's been sleeping in that cage for years. It isn't like he hates it.

That led to a whole somniferous riff on "What were they thinking?" Two of the more famous ones that came to mind were the 1985 introduction of New Coke and the 1968 Heidi Bowl (Google it, young readers.)

My list also included:

- The time a 16-year-old Fred sassed his 96-pound, four-foot-11-inch-tall mama in the kitchen. Mama, her arms elbow-deep in dishwater suds, nodded her head toward the dinner table and said, "Son, would you please hand me the plate off the table." Feeling his oats, six-foot-two Fred replied, "If you want the damn plate, get it yourself." Mama, not missing a beat, whirled around and slapped his face with the force of a freight train. She then turned calmly back to her task and repeated her request. Fred picked himself up from the linoleum floor, his cheek tattooed red with a small, wet handprint, and retrieved the plate.

- Cousin Queen Ester Campbell's third marriage. We sorta liked husbands No. 4 and 5. And, yes, Queen Ester is her given name. Her last name is the one frequently in question.

- That time we elected Warren G. Harding as 29th President of the United States. Ok, so I just broke my rule to remain apolitical. After all, President Harding did give us that infectious non-word, "normalcy," before he graciously up and died of a heart attack in 1923, two years into his first term.

- My brother Big G's basement stunt when he was 12. In a bit of circus showmanship for us younger kids, he tried walking on a cable spool turned on its side. He used a long, sharpened stick, pointy-side up, to steady himself as it rolled. When he predictably lost his balance, he fell forward and impaled the roof of his mouth with the stick. It was just one of many near-death experiences of his youth.

- The day Daddy brought home a used silver Buick Electra as a surprise for Mother. She did not want the car (I don't remember why), and apparently it had been a topic of a past conversation.

She refused to get in the car – ever – so Daddy drove it to work and back until he could unload it on a more welcoming household.

• The 1980s – Madonna mall hair. Enough said.

• My decision to defy my mother and shave my legs when I was 11. I guess the blondish stubble glinted in the light, because Mother rubbed her hand over my shin as soon as she saw it. I then tried lying, the prickly evidence notwithstanding. My punishment: I had to wear dresses to school for weeks so that everyone could admire my silky gams. It was shamefully out-of-fashion.

• That time before Aunt Sarah's funeral in South Georgia when Daddy remembered to return two bungie cords he had borrowed from Fred five months prior. We were standing in line for the visitation. After another out-of-town funeral – this time for Fred's mother – Daddy returned to us three Chinese take-out soup containers. We happened to be climbing into our car for the motorcade to the cemetery at the time. I suppose something about funerals makes Daddy want to square things up on this earth before departing it someday.

So, back to the big question: What were they thinking? Ultimately, I settled on this answer: They weren't.

Drunks, Fools and Chicken Salad Sammiches

When I was a teen, my mother would deposit me for a week at a time in Washington County, Alabama, to keep her widowed mother company. Grandmother, whom the locals reverently addressed as "Miss Genie," was legally blind. Glaucoma had robbed her of Agatha Christie mysteries and the countless other books that had been her escape while rearing 10 kids and passels of grandchildren on the family farm.

I stand corrected. She didn't rear kids, she reared children. "'Kids are baby goats,'" she'd say. She had been an English teacher before she married. She required proper English in her home. She also refused to use pet names for her children. When someone referred to her granddaughter Julia as "Julie," she would correct them on the spot. "'Julie' is the name of a mule," she'd say. "Her name is 'Jewel-e-a.'"

That's why her less-than-genteel language shocked me so much one day while we were sharing a chicken-salad "sammich" on her front-porch swing. She was recalling a recent telephone exchange. About midnight that night, the lone phone in her house buzzed three short times, signaling a call for her on the party line. She got out of bed, used the walls to navigate her way to the far end of the dark shot-gun house, and answered the phone.

"Hey, Miss Genie," drooled a drunken prankster. "Whatcha doin'?"

"Talking to a damn fool. But not for long!" she snapped, and hung up the phone.

I stopped swinging and stared at her, struck dumb by her use of a "cuss" word.

But in the ensuing years – including as recently as this very morning – I have found myself politely finishing conversations with, shall we say, people not blessed with much upstairs who compensate for it by being crazy. I always think about Miss Genie and her famous last words to the caller. Sometimes, profanity just fits. Perfectly.

Lest I get too smug casting judgment, I think back to an autumn Saturday a few years ago. I had invited a friend to the house for lunch, and drove across town that morning to a trendy deli to buy some gourmet chicken salad.

On the way home, I stopped in a supermarket parking lot to drop off some "slightly used" shoes in a donation bin. I grabbed the plastic bag off the seat and tossed the shoes into the hamper, listening with satisfaction as they hit the bottom.

When I got home, I opened the chicken-salad bag and discovered that my uppity entrée was in need of re-soling. Not only was I out a lunch, I had endangered everything else in the Hannah Home shed at the Piggly Wiggly. It was Indian summer, and if the mayo in that salad turned, well....

After several calls to the charity, I found a gentleman who would meet me at the box and rescue the bag. I think he really came just to take a look at the idiot who did the deed. Only a high dose of curiosity would have blasted a Southern man out of his Barcalounger on a football Saturday.

I'm quite certain I didn't disappoint. Flustered and embarrassed, I bumbled through an apology for interrupting his day and a proper show of gratitude for his kindness. I thought I saw a smile behind his clinched lips.

I'll bet you a chicken-salad sammich that when he answered his wife's pop quiz regarding the nutty call out, he unwittingly responded in pure Miss Genie fashion: "I was talking to a damn fool, but not for long. Bless her heart."

A Cattle Call for the Fat Farm

Gina Marie hit an all-time high on the sublime-to-ridiculous continuum last week. What tipped her over the top of the silly scale was a text inviting several of her weight-conscious girlfriends to join her in a Groupon deal for a fat farm retreat.

"1-Week Weight-Loss Retreat with Meals at The Biggest Loser Resort Niagara in Java Center, NY," read the offer. A regular $2,995 was slashed to $1,797 – a 40-percent discount!

"I want to do this. Like really," Gina Marie pleaded. While there certainly is nothing wrong with self-improvement and getting healthy, Gina Marie's urgency stems from having leapt from her signature size 0 to a whopping size 2. I think I was a size 2 for two days when I was, maybe, 10 years old?

The immediate response to her text was uncharacteristic silence. Imagine the chirping of cyber crickets. Most of us in the group chat could stand to lose a few pounds because of lives well led. Terri-Lyn had the convenient excuse of recent childbirth. But who pays almost $2,000 to go up north and starve when what we really need to do is dry out? Terri-Lyn excepted, bless her heart.

Finally, Sarah Witt couldn't stand the silence and threw a life raft to Gina Marie. "Puhleeaaseeee, Gina Marie!" Sarah Witt texted.

"I am the one who needs help! Wine is my downfall, but I guess I want it more than trying to look good. At my age, no one is looking anyway! They don't care if I am a heifer."

Sarah Witt was demonstrating the sublime Southern art form of self-deprecation. There is nothing bovine about this lovely woman. She was taking one for the team.

Then, emboldened by Sarah Witt's courage, but mistaking it for mine, Terri-Lyn came back a little too quickly with a reassuring, "Sister, you are so not a heifer!"

What? I was minding my own business when I got pulled into this little lovefest, and then got reassured that I am not, in fact, a cow. How does one respond? "Hey, Terri-Lyn, Sarah Witt is the heifer. Not me." No, that wouldn't work. I just decided to lie low and chew my cud.

But after a few seconds Terri-Lyn realized her misstep and the backpedaling began. "Oh! That was you, Sarah Witt – and you are not a heifer, either!" Too late. That dog done hunted.

She then tried a little desperate humor to advance the frozen clock. A self-deprecation Hail Mary. "I just throw my kids out front and hope folks look at them," she texted. Crickets again.

Sorry, Terri-Lyn, not biting. The chat stream ended abruptly. Not much else to say.

I'm giving Terri-Lyn a one-time mulligan for her sleep-deprived Mommy Brain. She really meant well, bless her heart (again). I'm actually too old, and care too little, to get worked up about the cattle call. Besides, we've all had those disastrous moments of innocently throwing a turd in the punch bowl.

I've congratulated a poochy woman on her upcoming blessing, and asked more than one mature gentleman to introduce me to his daughter when he was escorting a nubile young date. Then there was the wart I tried to brush off a new friend's chin. You just can't dig out of those moments. Best to move on, for everyone's sake. "How 'bout dem Braves?" is a favorite subject-changer around here.

As for Gina Marie, she got no takers on her Groupon offer. I doubt she'll go alone. It's a girl thing. If she does, the rest of us will hold up our wine glasses in tribute. "You go, girl!" Then we'll toast to something else. Like dryer lint.

Angler Triplets Tell All, Almost

Whether true or stretched to the point of absurdity, most fish tales begin after the catch is reeled in. Southern men, storytellers by birthright, tend to stretch their fish tales and associated fish tails longer in direct proportion to the stretch of time between the catching and the telling.

If you are a true Woman of the South, you know to let the guys have their moments of glory – it doesn't cost you anything but a straight face. Besides, we'll reciprocate when we tell them how little we spent on whatever we had to have at the mall last week.

But my husband's most outlandish fish tale began a couple hundred miles north of the spot where the first line was cast. I know some of it to be true, because I bore witness.

A few years ago, a couple of buddies invited Fred to go fishing with them on the Apalachicola coast. It was not their first trip to the Florida Panhandle, so Fred knew that while some fishing would be involved, there would also be plenty of opportunities for fresh oysters, Jack Daniels and whopper tales. Fishing was somewhat secondary to the true goal – a guy trip with Road Rules in place.

On day one of the big adventure, Fred was up and ready early, fishing gear and overnight bag by the front door. He paced with anticipation like a kid waiting for the last school bell of the year, glancing frequently out the front door to watch for the carpool's arrival.

As always, Fred was the snappy dresser. He donned a sea-foam green Columbia fishing shirt, cut out in back; sand-colored khaki shorts and a pair of deck shoes. I was amused by his anticipation and equally looking forward to three days of sole possession of the TV clicker.

When the SUV pulled up, Fred was out the door lickety split. But a few minutes later, he was back with buddy Darwin, both belly laughing. "We need you to take a picture," Fred said to me. I soon saw what was so funny. He and Darwin were dressed identically. Same exact shirt, same khakis, same deck shoes, same white hair.

I started chuckling. "You haven't seen all of it, yet," they said, and pulled me outside. Standing by the SUV was the third muske-teer, Joe Mac, who had also gotten the dress memo. His uniform matched theirs, from the white mop down to the deck shoes.

I snapped a photo of the angler triplets, and off they went. Bless their hearts.

In the same situation, any true Woman of the South would have died before being seen in the same get-up as her sisters. It wasn't a problem for the guys until they drove up to their favorite break-fast place down the road. "We're not going in like this," Joe Mac said. But Fred insisted, and got his way.

"So we went into this establishment, and everyone's head turned," he told me later.

An excited waitress asked, "Are you professional fishermen?"

"Yes, we are," Darwin said. "We belong to the Apalachicola Fishing Club, and we are headed down to a tournament."

The tale stretched bigger as the road home stretched further away. They stopped in a barbecue restaurant at the state line, and by this time, they were Southeast Division Champion fishermen competing to defend their hard-earned title for the third time. I think they even signed a few autographs.

Fred said the fishing that trip was lousy. But the tale of the three amigos grows longer each time he tells it. I just smile to myself.

That Kind of Friend

After my brother died last summer, my dear friend Jennifer Ann drove all the way from Memphis just to check on me. She couldn't make the funeral, so she day-tripped on Saturday, bringing with her tales of our youth that tickled my daughter and pulled a few laughs out of me when I didn't have any to give.

Jennifer Ann is *that* kind of friend. Our antics date back to fourth grade, when she moved to The Mountain from Georgia. We became fast friends – same age, same neighborhood, same church. Her sense of humor was laced with sarcasm, which was quite fun until you were the target. I generally gave as good as I got, and together, we were a force.

When we were 12, we went down to the creek behind her house and followed it fearlessly to a storm-sewer pipe. We crab-crawled through the tunnel, ducking spider webs and straddling the standing water. I always thought the iridescent rings of purple, red and orange afloat in the creek were beautiful, like Carnival glass. Who knew they were pools of emulsified tree rot, oil runoff and other deposits? Sewer-crawling was what kids did. It was pub-crawling boot camp, only barefoot.

When safely downstream, we perched on a rock and took our first puff of a cigarette. I about choked up a lung. Two drags did it for me. I think Jennifer Ann was more adventurous, but she didn't make a habit of it, either.

When we shared an apartment our senior year of college, Jennifer Ann bought a parakeet without the blessing of her parents. She asked me to feign ownership of the bird when parent weekend brought her folks to visit. That was just a hint of things to come.

After I graduated, I got a job in our college town. Jennifer Ann had a few more classes to finish, so she moved in with me in my yuppie flat. A few weeks later she brought home a St. Bernard puppy, again without parental nod. This was problematic because they would be housing her menagerie for the next three years when Jennifer Ann moved home and went to law school.

The bird was no big deal. But that puppy! My apartment had no backyard, so we had to keep it in our bathroom while we were out. Doing what puppies do, Abby chewed up the base end of my bathroom cabinet. That's when we discovered the magic properties of wood filler.

One October day, I came home to find Jennifer Ann hysterical and Abby panicked, her head stuck in a small plastic pumpkin. The puppy was tossing her head to and fro and howling all the world like a four-legged headless horseman. Bless her heart. Jennifer Ann was about to call the fire department when I brandished some scissors and carefully extracted Abby's head, which emerged sweat-drenched but otherwise unscathed.

We were each other's maid of honor when that time came, and our daughters were born six weeks apart. Jennifer Ann had moved to Memphis by then, and we went about our adult lives with only the occasional gift of time together.

Jennifer Ann and I don't talk that often, but when we do, it's like we were never apart. She has had a full life, a successful career, a beautiful daughter and three St. Bernards in the years since our girlhood, and I love hearing about all of her adventures.

What I love most is that she's there, without prompting, when I need her, regardless. And I'm there for her, with my pumpkin-carving scissors ready to go. She's *that* kind of friend.

Where the Deer and the Jackalope Roam

The jackalope lost its place as the strangest trophy in our home office when Max arrived. Mythical creatures first "sighted" in Wyoming (think Bigfoot), jackalopes are jackrabbits with antelope horns. Ours is an eBay find from an enterprising taxidermist. On the other hand, Max is the real deal. I should know. I shot him.

After moving to East Alabama, I wanted to earn a little "street cred" – or, more aptly, "dirt-trail cred" – from my brethren at work. I beseeched my buddy Jabbo, a state-champion bow hunter and expert marksman, to teach me to hunt and help me snag an eight-point buck.

I think Jabbo was honored to serve as missionary in the conversion of a life-long manicured suburbanite whose Cro-Magnon meals depended on the butcher at the Piggly Wiggly. And so began the Great Deer Hunt of 2008-09.

First step was target practice on Jabbo's land, a woodsy paradise complete with a cozy cabin he hand-built for his family – wife, Markel, and 12-year-old daughter, Katy-Bug. Markel and Katy-Bug are both crack shots themselves, each with more than one trophy buck watching over their family room. Markel graciously offered up her Remington 700 7mm-08 rifle for my use in pursuit of The Buck.

We got down to the real business at hand Christmas week. First day, Jabbo instructed me to wash my hair and lather up with Dead Downwind shampoo. If your teenager needs an acne astringent, look no further.

Garbed in camo overalls, jacket and Muck boots, cap covering my straw-like hair, I looked like a sovereign-citizen wannabe trekking around the Alabama woods that are my birthright. Well, sorta. I was born in Georgia. I'll strive to keep the facts straight in case any birthers read this and see a false claim for what it is.

Always a gentleman, Jabbo declined to expose me to his hunting club and associated conditions. So the first day he took me to a claustrophobic shooting house in a nearby wood, where we sat on our haunches for several hours with nary a deer in our sights.

I think Jabbo was more disappointed than I was. "Miss Sister," he said, "I've seen dozens of 'em down this way in the last few weeks. I can't believe our luck."

After another pre-dawn start that led to naught, we called a holiday truce to focus on the Immaculate Birther and then on New Year's festivities. But when all the dead spruce trees went curbside, out came the camo and the scent-stripping shampoo again.

This time, we tried a late-afternoon approach. Before dusk on Jan. 9, we hit the trail again, deer scat (droppings) as our guide. Jabbo had talked a neighbor into letting him hang a tree stand on the outskirts of a virgin hayfield, where the deer roamed free and plentiful. I needed all the handicaps I could get.

Jabbo waxed philosophical as we trekked to our perch about "the peacefulness of being one with nature," yada, yada, yada. The air was colder than a frozen turkey. I was just ready to feel my toes again.

Once in the stand, though, Jabbo was all business. Silently, he scouted the edges of the field through his rifle scope, signaling when he spotted several deer out of range. He showed only slight irritation when his radio crackled to let him know Markel was in position at another prime hunting spot nearby.

I finally caught the spirit of the moment, but I also felt guilty that my bucket-list quest was interrupting Jabbo's family time and his own hunting season. Bless his heart.

I was soon thrilled to see two doe scamper into the open, playing awhile before retreating. Then out came my buck. His profile was majestic, rack impressive. (Insert cleavage joke here.) I knew he was mine from the start, and I carefully took aim and fired. The bullet whizzed above his head. Not recognizing the sound or its origin, he just looked around, confused.

"Miss Sister, you might want to wait a minute to see if it's a trophy," Jabbo cautioned when the buck looked our way. Too late. Blood lust won out and I fired again, this time hitting the buck right behind the shoulder. Down he went, and Jabbo and I stared, amazed. Then another shot rang us back to the present, and Markel radioed that she thought she had hit something.

Jabbo drove his pickup as close as he could to my buck, grabbed its back legs, and with a grunt, tossed the 175-pound carcass onto the tailgate. I hopped into the truck bed, held up the deer's head and posed for a photo with my trophy – a mutant specimen that sported one full antler and one nub. I had thinned the herd and improved its gene pool.

Jabbo spared me the ritual smearing of blood on my face, partly out of respect, but mostly because we needed to beat a trail to find Markel and help her track her wounded prey. Once we rendezvoused, I wimpishly accepted an offer by Jabbo's father to tote me back to my car on his Gator while Jabbo and Markel stayed on the trail.

I later emailed the prize photo to my friend Shannon, mostly for shock effect. It worked.

"Oh my goodness," she replied. "You shot Max!" It took me a minute to get the reference to the animated dog in How the Grinch Stole Christmas. The Grinch strapped one antler to Max's head before he hitched him to his sleigh and carted off all the presents from Whoville.

Yep, Shannon nailed it. I shot Max.

Jabbo later delivered to me a freezer-load of venison and a European mount (skull and antler only) of my trophy, which Fred hung on the wall by the jackalope.

It's about time to hang a Christmas ornament on Max's antler and raise my annual toast to Jabbo, who made me appreciate the art of the hunt, the savory goodness of deer sausage and a warm home in winter. Oh, and hair conditioner.

Gold, Frankincense and Miracles

The Wise Man who meant to present Daddy and Mother with gifts of gold, frankincense and myrrh at our Christmas celebration last weekend had a brilliant idea, but it dulled flat in delivery. The giver, Golden Boy, was so enchanted with his idea that he planned to repeat it at a second family gathering the following day. That proved his undoing.

The confusion on Daddy's face upon opening packages of Gold-Toe-brand socks and gilded playing cards became even more pronounced when Mother fought her way through layers of stubborn bubble wrap to find two vials of myrrh essential oils. Bless their hearts.

Back home, waiting for day two, were similar "gold" trinkets and two vials of frankincense.

Though the intended gifts would have been, shall we say -- cute and clever -- Golden Boy's botched delivery made the rest of us roll with laughter.

It was good medicine.

We were valiantly trying to carry on our family traditions in spite of the first-year absence of my brother James, who I'm certain was hooting with us from heaven. The Gifts of the Magi could have come right out of his Santa bag.

But another gift that came to us six months ago has been the true salve for our wounds. Especially for Mother and Daddy.

Last spring, Mother's great niece Kasi moved to The Mountain with her husband Brennan, newly transferred from another state by his employer. Kasi was "great with child," and her mother – my first cousin – was equally great with anxiety over the young couple's leaving their support system at such a critical time.

My cousin called in the cavalry -- her Aunt Libby (Mother) – and the problem was solved. Mother is strong as flint when you need help, and a bowlful of jelly when it comes to the grandkids. Perfect combo for the situation at hand.

When I was expecting her first grandchild (Little Darlin'), Mother had declared that she would be called "Grandmother" by her progeny. But she made the mistake of bouncing Little Darlin' on her knees and singing "Be-bop-a-lu-la, she's my baby," to her one time too many.

Little Darlin' started calling her "Bebop," and so she was. The Glacier melted, and global warming had nothing to do with it. She has been Bebop now to seven grandkids, their friends and parents, and half The Mountain. Her car tag declares it to the other half.

Bebop's youngest grandchildren are now 15, so it's been quite a spell since she had a baby to cuddle. So when Kasi's little Meredith was born six months ago, Bebop quickly became a surrogate grandmother, complete with all the spoils.

"Where's My Baby?" Bebop hollered out the front door as Kasi, Brennan and Meredith pulled in the driveway Saturday. When they entered, that baby lit up the room like a Yule log. I don't think her little bottom hit the floor twice over the afternoon, such were the snuggles.

Brennan joined in the word game that proved challenging for those of us of a certain generation, current pop references being prominent clues. We older folks got even when the Rook cards came out.

This year we didn't miss the little impish tree that usually sits at Bebop and Granddaddy's front door, coming alive with a "Merry Christmas" when we approach and scaring the devil out of us.

This year we didn't miss the strange little package that would start convulsing and yelling, "Help! Help! Get me out of here," when we opened presents. (I'm not asking where those sons-of-Furby disappeared to. Just thankful they did.)

This year we did miss James more than anyone let on, stiff upper lips and all that. But Bebop's Christmas Baby, the Gifts of the Magi – and a whole lot of grace – made this a most joyous holiday for a family who needed one.

May that grace and the miracle of new birth extend to you and yours this season.

Merry Christmas.

She's Come Undone

Recently, I slipped down into the suds of my garden tub to soak in the soothing words of a podcast on "The Power of Vulnerability." But I Suwannee, you're never more vulnerable than when a crazed jet tub defies death and threatens to suck you into a bubble vortex.

And trust me – at that moment, you don't hold any power.

The Incident of my Undoneness began exactly 3:08 minutes into the presenter's profound insights on the benefits of exposing your flank. With more than 28 million views, this 20-minute jewel surely held the keys to the enlightenment kingdom. It also was about the longest time a tub of hot water would stay hot.

So I connected my IPhone to my handy portable Bluetooth wireless speaker for enhanced sound quality. I then propped up the phone on the tub deck – away from any threat of water damage, but close enough to see the video.

"By the time you're a social worker for 10 years, what you realize is that connection is why we're here," said the author and research professor. "It's what gives purpose and meaning to our lives."

Ooh, this is good stuff, I thought, sinking deeper into the water infused with the aroma-therapeutic qualities of essential oils and a milk bath product. Fred was co-medicating in another room with a beer and an NFL playoff game.

The presenter went on to reveal that shame unravels connection. She defined shame as something about a person that, if others knew it or saw it, would make that person unworthy of connection. "The thing that underpinned this was excruciating vulnerability," she said. "This idea of, in order for connection to happen, we have to allow ourselves to be seen, really seen."

That was about the moment I turned on the air jets in the tub. Connection really happened exactly 5:25 into the show.

This requires a bit of background… About 10 years ago, Fred and I decided to install a jet tub in the master bath. When I went to pick out a tub at our local plumbing fixture store, the saleswoman talked me into buying a model with air jets instead of water jets.

"It's the latest thing," she said with gusto. "Everybody loves them." She leaned toward me, true concern for my health furrowing her brow, and jiggled her lure. "The air circulators don't carry all those icky standing-water germs you find in water jets." I bit – hook, line and sinker.

Okay. I was an idiot. How's that for vulnerability?

At the time, it sounded great. All things being equal, who wouldn't opt for better sanitation? And it wasn't like I could sample the floor model or take one home for a "try-on."

But after installing our technologically superior porcelain body basin, we soon discovered that the jet pressure would barely budge from all-out pelting, despite attempts to regulate it. It left you in welts and shot water into the air and over the tub edges like a geyser.

I rarely fought the battle of the jets, especially when the whole purpose of a bath was to lower my stress level. But occasionally I got lured back in, especially when I listened to psycho-insights into the meaning of life or world peace. The jets would work better this time. No reason to let the past inform the present. I was like the kid who licked the frozen flag pole.

So I pushed the button to turn on the jets. The air exploded underneath the surface, erupting into two-foot water spouts and exponentially expanding the milk bath bubbles in seconds. I pushed the button again to tamp down the pressure. Nothing. Then I pushed the off button. Nothing. Then I threw a towel over the IPhone to protect it from further water assault, and tried several more times to turn off the jets. Nothing.

With both arms outstretched, I tried to corral the foam back into the confines of the tub. Again I pushed the button, using a different finger, at a different angle. Nothing.

Finally, I had to allow myself to be seen – really seen. Boy, do I hate pulling out the helpless woman card. It really chaps my rear. "Fred!" I yelled, hoping he would hear me above Terry Bradshaw and the blasting air jets. "Fred! Come here, please! I need you."

I simultaneously began draining the tub and running clean water to wash the bubbles off my body, which by now resembled the Michelin Man's babe, and truly expose my flank and my rear.

The killer tub quickly evoked a full-blown Fred Fit when my prince could not tame the beast. He made three trips down to the basement breaker box to shut off the power, the third try finally bringing the bubble monster to a gurgling death.

We retreated, psychologically wounded, back to our respective corners.

"I know that vulnerability is the core of shame and fear and our struggle for worthiness, but it appears that it's the birthplace of joy, of creativity, of belonging, of love," Professor Touchy-Feely continued, totally unperturbed by The Incident of My Undoneness. Bless her heart.

The secret to fulfillment, she concluded at 19:01, is to love with our whole hearts and "to let ourselves be seen, deeply seen, vulnerably seen."

Mission accomplished.

Two Scooby-Doo Sheets to the Wind? If Only...

"Whatchall doing Friday night?" Lindy asked innocently enough.

Not thinking, I answered truthfully, "Nothing." And that, dear readers, is how Fred and I found ourselves sitting on a picnic bench freezing our fannies off while celebrating the Jewish Feast of Tabernacles under a front-porch tent fashioned from 1970s Scooby-Doo bedsheets.

It was fall 1999, and Lindy lived next door to us on The Mountain in a ramshackle do-it-yourselfer that needed to be done in. We were merely "waving neighbors," so her question caught me off guard during a mail-box chat.

Oh, and did I mention Fred was scheduled for hernia-repair surgery that next Monday? Nursing a side stitch while sitting on a back-less, hard bench was fresh hell for him.

The fact that this past Sunday – New Year's Day – marked our 20th anniversary tells you all you need to know about Fred. Bless his sweet, forgiving heart. That fateful night 17-plus years ago also led us to establish a hard-fast marital rule that has served us well ever since. More on that later.

When extending her invitation, Lindy explained that she celebrated Jewish holidays "to feel closer to Jesus." That was a new one on me, but I have since learned it's common practice in several Christian denominations. Just not the Baptist church we called home. But I was game.

The Feast of Tabernacles – "Sukkot" – is more literally translated "Feast of Booths," referring to the temporary shelters of the Israelites during their 40 years of wandering in the desert. It commemorates their historical Exodus from Egypt, and their dependence on God (Leviticus 23:42-43). It is also a thanksgiving harvest festival.

That may be why Lindy served a traditional American Thanksgiving dinner that evening. In addition to Fred and me, guests included two women and a youth minister from Lindy's church, who was to officiate.

While we waited for the extremely late "rabbi," one of the women discussed her preparations for the End of Days, which she was certain was just weeks away at the turn of the Millennium. I had to wonder why she was wasting one of her last free evenings with us.

When the rabbi finally arrived, he sat at the head of the table and donned a yarmulke. Good-sport Fred capped his bare head, too. Oh, to have had a camera phone.

After the ceremony, we bit into dressing so salty it must have been made from cornbread and Dead Sea water. The rabbi got real red wine in a real glass goblet. Grape juice in Solo cups for the rest of us. There were no Canaan wedding miracles to be had on The Mountain.

While I washed down the dressing with grape juice, I felt something furry rub against my shins. One of Lindy's 13 cats had joined us in the tent to sample the turkey. It got more than its share of mine, especially after I noticed a feline hair nestled in the gravy.

Walking gingerly across the dark rocky yards to the refuge of our own front door that night, I clutched Fred's elbow while he clutched his herniated side. With a new appreciation for the Israelites' Red Sea crossing to freedom, I apologized to Fred nine ways from Sunday and vowed to never, ever, again make a commitment for us without consulting him. He made the same promise.

So if you offer me two free tickets to watch Alabama play for the national championship in Hawaii -- along with a two-week vacation at a five-star Maui hotel -- don't be surprised if I answer, "Let me check with Fred first." That promise has stuck.

And speaking of vows, Fred and I started our second 20 years doing what we did on our wedding day – getting blessed by our preacher and going home to watch football. It worked so well the first time, we figured, why mess with a good thing? Unless, of course, Scooby-Doo sheets are involved.

One Flew Over My Cuckoo's Nest

Golden Boy walked for his college diploma last weekend, bringing an end to 22 years of raising the baby bird and preparing him to fly. And off he flew – to Ireland and Germany for master's degree work studying supply chain management, data analytics and other stuff the Mercedes folks know better than most.

Me, I got the Mother's Day gift of a lifetime – a magna cum laude civil engineer (notice how I slid that in) – and yet another chance to be his personal secretary. He graduated Friday night, spent Saturday packing and drove home Sunday so that Fred and I could baby-sit his car and give him personal cab service to the Atlanta airport.

GB's parting words: "Mom, I need you to mail back the key to my apartment, so I don't get fined." Which, correctly interpreted, means that if I don't take care of this while the baby is traipsing around Irish pubs and German beer halls, my account will take the hit.

Then there was, "Oh, and I lost a couple of credit cards the other day. I looked for them, but didn't find them. I think they fell out of my wallet." Interpretation: He looked through the pockets of two pairs of khaki shorts, didn't see them and didn't have time to fool with the folly of such trivial matters as his mother's credit rating when there were illegal graduation night fireworks parties to attend.

I spent Monday mailing back keys, reporting lost credit cards and, oh yes, paying his MBA summer tuition bill that was due ASAP. After having received the bill electronically three weeks ago, he thought to send it to me all the way from Dublin, mostly because he received an email threatening cancellation of his summer classes.

Yes, I am guilty of pandering to one of those monster millennials our generation has produced. But, there are deeper motivations at play here – payback and maternal guilt. And, of course, they stem from a childhood experience.

When Golden Boy was seven, one of his class assignments was to dress as an historical figure and give a little presentation.

Ever the over-compensating working mom, I helped him assemble his costume. He wanted to be Hercules. It just so happened that we already had on hand (don't ask why) a little toga with purple overlay, gold-braided tassel belt and laurel wreath, so we used that as a starting point.

On dress-up day, which I had efficiently marked on my calendar lest it slip away from memory, I helped him put on his toga and Teva sandals and watched proudly from the front porch as he marched the block to his elementary school and crossed the street, flagged by the safety patrol.

I looked forward all day to hearing how well it went, confident that I would get the appropriate thank-you as his costumer-in-chief with a chatty debriefing of Hercules' debut. "How'd dress-up day go?" I asked as soon as I saw him.

"It's tomorrow," he said, in monotone, and said no more. Bless his heart.

So when he walked across the university coliseum stage to the applause of parents, fellow graduates and other folks ready for the pomp to end and the parties to begin, I couldn't help thinking about the first time he walked for academia in a cap (okay, fine, twig-wreath) and gown. It made me smile.

His cold-served revenge this week was mild, and my guilt assuaged by my penance.

Oh, and I cancelled his credit cards. The baby bird has flown.

Thou Shalt Not Inhale

One of the first times smoke on the mountain caused a bit of a stir was back in Exodus, when God blanketed Mount Sinai with a pillar of the stuff before calling Moses up to receive the The Law carved in stone. The smoke served as a warning sign for the Israelites to stay back lest they perish.

Ten "Thou Shalts" and a few millennia later, the wafting smoke on the mountain didn't warn those nearby. It just triggered an alarm that sent them out into the cold and put the Baptist deacons responsible for it in a bit of a pickle.

The deacons, who shall remain nameless here but not before God, were taking their monthly turn at watching over the down-and-out men sheltered overnight at a local men's mission on The Mountain where I'm from. I have a first-person account from one of the deacons, who happens to share half my DNA.

Another church was responsible for cooking and serving the evening meal, and four men from our church took over from there, Mr. Nameless explained.

"Our duties were to check the men in, collect all their medicines and occasional pocket knives until morning, make sure they cleaned up the place after their dinner," and see to it they tucked themselves into the cots lining the long wall of the communal bedroom, he said.

The deacons would arise early the next morning and cook a big breakfast – toast, bacon, eggs and coffee – then wake their charges up in time to serve them and send them on their way by 8 a.m. The church team would then clean up, and the team captain would write a report on anything that needed relaying to the full-time day workers coming in after their departure.

This particular night shift provided a bit more detail for the report than normal, on account of that alarm.

After the homeless men had gone down for the night, the deacons went to the Upper Room and settled around the table for a little five-card draw. In their defense, there was no television, and it wasn't a Sunday or a Wednesday night.

All would have been kosher had even one of the card players noticed the smoke alarm on the ceiling directly above the poker table.

"Suddenly, smoke from the cigarettes set off the alarm, awoke all the 'guests' and, by rule, forced everyone to evacuate the building in the middle of the night," Mr. Nameless recalled. The weather was cold, and some of the evacuees were "sort of scantily clad." Bless their hearts.

Compounding the chaos was the troublesome finding that none of the guilty knew how to turn off the alarm. "Our captain walked a block or so to a fire station to ask them to turn off the alarm," Mr. Nameless said. "They informed him they couldn't do so unless he returned to the site of the alarm and notified them by telephone."

So he crawfished back to the mission – avoiding the hard, red eyes of his shivering wards, and made the call. A fireman then came over and disengaged the alarm. The silver lining of that cloud of smoke was that at least the fire department hadn't sent a ladder truck racing over with sirens blaring.

Daddy -- I mean, Mr. Nameless -- said the errant deacons didn't get relieved of their duties, but they never played poker at the mission again.

As for that written report, it included one new recommendation that was carved in stone henceforth:

Thou shalt not drag and puff in the mission.

Gonged, but not Forgotten

The death bell tolled at ABC this season. It reverberated in the deep tones of a gong. No one, I reckon, should be shocked at the reincarnation of yet another mid-1970s cheesy production, but I thought the network geniuses would put at least a modicum of decent distance between the passing of original Gong Show creator Chuck Barris (1929 – 2017) and the resurrection of his baby.

Such are the desperate times in which network TV lives – survives at least – with the aid of a respirator and the rehashing of old programming.

The original NBC version of the amateur talent show, which ran from 1976 – 1980, was at least novel, and had a few notably funny segments – the Unknown Comic being my personal favorite.

With a brown paper bag over his head, the Unknown Comic appeared on stage, dished out a couple of awful jokes, then disappeared. It was all so bad that it was, well, good. Like watching a train wreck or listening to Mary Nell Simpson lisp through "Sweet, Sweet Spirit" in Sunday worship service.

The revival Gong Show did bring me a little amusement, though, as it reminded me fondly of another atrocity from the original show's era that came from my own creative labors: The Unknown Nude.

Back when cavemen were discovering flint, I was studying painting in pursuit of an undergrad minor in art. We were learning to paint the human figure, and a New Jersey law student named Margret was our subject matter. Her accent didn't give her away. In fact, I'm not sure I ever heard her talk. I knew she was a Yankee the minute I got a gander at her unshaven gams.

The professor confirmed my suspicions when he introduced her, in silken bathrobe, to his class of nine young co-eds and one poor mama's boy who promptly turned crimson up to his Bama ball cap. The professor then assigned Margret to step onto a butcher-paper-covered riser at the center of the studio.

The brunette model disrobed and dropped her lumpy fanny into a chair draped in artsy fabric. She positioned her legs about 18 inches apart, and – yes – the sun shone where it really shouldn't oughta. Ever. She placed her upper limbs on the arm rests, glanced at us distractedly and then looked off into the distance just as comfy as you please. Probably reviewing Marbury v. Mason in her head.

Mama's Boy quickly claimed a spot for his easel behind her as far as he could get and still have some reference point on which to focus his brush strokes. The rest of us, a little slower on the uptake, then staked out similar real estate. I jockeyed for a partial side view, which included no bottom parts but both breasts. Best I could do under the circumstances.

Then we painted.

Every class day, Margret would re-emerge from the bathroom in her kimono, disrobe and plant her feet in the magic marker outlines the teacher had drawn around them on day one. Finally, our hell was over, and I had a 30x36-inch albatross in blue undertones to show for it.

That summer, when I settled in back at my parents' house on The Mountain, I brought Margret (the painting) with me. But Mother gonged her. "I'll not have that trash under my roof, 'art or no art'," she proclaimed. I think if Margret's underarm pits had been a little seemlier, Mother might have relented.

So I toted Margret over to the Phillips' house, our high school hang-out. There, she was welcomed and celebrated by all who got a view.

When Margret debuted at "The Ps'," the original Gong Show was off the air, but still fresh on our minds. So in tribute to the Unknown Comic, and to hide her butt-ugly face, my friends propped Margret up on a table, cut the sides out of a paper bag, and placed it over her head. She was then forever dubbed, "Margret, the Unknown Nude."

Margret stayed in her place of honor the entire summer, until I could haul her back to school and then on to closets in the many abodes I have had since.

When Fred first saw her, he added a new nickname, "One Hung Low," because, as I said, I was at a funny angle when I laid brush to canvas, and I painted what I saw. Bless her heart.

In later years, we dressed Margret up more than once in pretty Christmas wrap and hauled her to dirty Santa parties, only to have her swing back our way before the party ended or in the ensuing year.

She now gathers dust in our basement, stacked I'm sure with some other butt-ugly pieces I produced in those years. But now that The Gong Show is back on the screen, and tacky is back en vogue, Margret may be making an appearance at a Christmas party near you....

Red Hats and Greenhouses

Golden Boy had quite the dilemma deciding on a retirement gift for me that didn't suggest I am about to make that final trek into the wilderness to prop my old bones up against a big tree and wither away.

Or fade away like an old soldier. Or wear purple and join a Red Hat Club. Or, to borrow a quote from our five-year-old granddaughter, "Sissy, you disappeared out of nowhere."

You see, I am retiring next month from my "day job" at a fairly young age – as these things go – and I hope I have many years ahead, and at least a half tank of gas left in my engine. There are things to do, people to see, columns to write, mountains to climb. Well, maybe not mountains. I do have this trick-knee-thing going on.

"I thought about getting you a rocking chair," GB shared with me a few days ago. "But that seemed to suggest you were really old." Bless his heart. He's quite the expert at earning brownie points.

"At one store, I saw a huge wine glass that had 'I'm retired' etched on it," he added. "But I didn't want to imply you were just going to drink yourself to death." Good save, son. (Now, why would that even cross his mind? Hmm.)

As the baby in the family, GB had already contributed a lot to my ability to start a new season. He earned his Master of Business Administration in May, ending more than three decades of educational fees of one kind or another for Fred and me. Four kids, four college graduates. Our biggest point of pride.

Way back when, when GB graduated from day care into kindergarten, we shifted his tuition payment to a lake house payment and broke even. This graduation was even sweeter than that! It was one of the final boxes I had to check so that I could retire and continue to enjoy the lifestyle to which I've become accustomed. Or, to quote a great philosopher, the late actor Max Asnas, "Money is something you got to make in case you don't die."

I always wanted to leave work on my own terms – or to quote another great thinker, Author Unknown – "The best time to start thinking about your retirement is before the boss does."

To keep GB from wasting more time pondering token gifts for his mama, I gave him the opportunity to give me something I really wanted, and to get some personal use out of his shiny new civil engineering degree and MBA before an employer put them to work.

I asked him to design and build a greenhouse for me, gardening being on my list of Things I Plan to Do When I Retire. He jumped at the project, to my delight. He did some online research, and we visited a neighbor's greenhouse to get ideas.

But before we could get much further into the project, San Antonio called. GB had a phone interview, then the company flew him out to inspect him in the flesh. Three weeks after he ended his college career, he was hired to start his work career.

That was the best retirement gift of all. I passed the baton. My real work here is done. Time to put on my red hat and disappear out of nowhere.

She Who Laughs Last, Bwahaha...

An obituary recently posted on social media has given Little Darlin' new hope that she might finally have the last word with me. That's because Southern moms don't like sass. Teenaged daughters can't exist without it. The combo is as explosive as a July 4th trailer park fireworks show after an Alabama-Georgia border run to Crazy Joe's.

When I read the Cincinnati Enquirer homage written by the deceased's son, I sent it to Little Darlin'. "The gauntlet has been thrown down," I challenged. "I hope you have many more years to gather material."

The bereft son listed among his mother's survivors "a mentally deranged Chihuahua [yes, dear readers, that's redundant].... and a house full of stuff we have no idea what to do with." He noted his mother's many talents, the greatest of which was "helicopter parenting." And, he ended, "A table of Mom's treasured collection will be set out for people to choose from and take mementos. Seriously, please take her stuff. We're up to our eyeballs in Christmas wreaths."

Lest I feel too smug regarding the funeral-home flea-market concept, I quickly remembered my own dear mother recently bringing me a beyond-the-pale hat once owned by our late second cousin 'Becca Louise. True to her raisin', 'Becca Lou wore a hat to church every Sunday of her adult life. Her collection was as legendary as it was gaudy. After she passed, all her 300-plus hats went to church with her one last time, so that her loved ones could select their favorite to take home and enjoy. Thanks, Mother, for thinking of me.

But, back to last words. Responding to my online challenge a little too quickly for my comfort, Little Darlin' replied within seconds. "Already on it," she said.

Then she railed off some of the more colorful things that would probably make the tribute. "The word 'tump,' purple hats, 'The Curling Iron Incident of 1997,' bird-feeders, Ella Fitzgerald and that time you gave me a copy of 'Lean In' for Christmas."

Before I could reply, she went on to post to voyeurs of our witty repartee, "For those of you unfamiliar with The Curling Iron Incident of 1997, I would like to clarify that it WAS an accident, but I do still have scars (a tiny one behind my right ear and an emotional one)."

Milk it, sister, milk it, I thought. But, her hair did look adorable in those curls. Did I mention that her caller ID tag for me is "Mother Superior?" I'm sure it was once "Mommie Dearest," but she is softening a bit as the scars recede.

I don't think I'd be generalizing to suggest that all Southern women have emotional scars that involve their mothers and their hair -- with most occurring on a Saturday night or Sunday morning. My personal trauma is a nightmare recollection of noxious Toni home perms and wet hair slimed in Dippity Do, wound tightly around spike rollers impaled into my head with Bobby pins and sealed for overnight baking under a pair of Mother's nylon panties.

Maybe 'Becca-Lou started wearing those hats after her mother created one-too-many church-day atrocities atop her young head, bless her heart.

Little Darlin' went on with a teaser for our sideline readers: "You'll have to wait for a more detailed account until Mama buys the farm. I can't be revealing all my best material."

Oh, yeah? I'll come back and haint you like a deranged Chihuahua capped in nylon panties, eyes ablaze through the leg holes. Why? 'Cause I said so. And that's the last word.

But, Seriously! About the Author

Julia Harwell Segars in a 1984 magna cum laude graduate of the University of Alabama, with a Bachelor of Arts degree in journalism and a minor in graphic design.

Her early career included two years as a news reporter for The Tuscaloosa News before joining a Fortune 500 company headquartered in Birmingham, AL, as a writer in their public relations department. She later served as editor of the company's four-color monthly magazine; then became a manager in employee communications and services, with oversight for all internal publications, plus audio-visual services that included a business television network.

During those years, Julia received numerous top awards in business writing, editing and overall publication quality from the International Association of Business Communicators at the local, Southeast regional and international levels.

She went on to various other leadership positions in the company in line operations and human resources before her election by the company's board of directors in 2002 as vice president and regional chief information officer. She spent the last 11 years of her corporate career in Anniston, AL, as division vice president of customer service operations for 12 counties in East Alabama.

In 2008, she led a creative team in the production of the book Dear Dani©, a collection of advice letters from 56 prominent women in East Alabama to the generation coming behind them. Profits from sales of Dear Dani were used to provide scholarships to area female college students in a state-wide leadership development program tailored for them.

After 31 years in corporate life, Julia retired in July 2017 to return her focus to writing and other creative pursuits as owner of Segars Creative, LLC.

She began writing Aunt Sister columns for the Talladega Daily Home in 2016 as a soft launch into her second career, and was delighted that the Alabama Press Association found her work worthy of a first-place award for humor columns in its 2017 Better Newspapers Contest.

She is even more appreciative that reader response has been so positive, and hopes this collection of columns is equally well-received.